Recommendations for Held in His Hands...

Sue Boldt confronts fear, hope, and healing in this remarkably short volume. Her sweet mix of theology and experience will bolster your faith, no matter what you face. Having walked the cancer road with my wife, I especially appreciate the wise words of a woman who we've watched grow from an enthusiastic Christian teen to an established leader in His church.

Ralph Moore
Hope Chapel Founder
Exponential Leader

Held in His Hands *is not just a book but rather the inked words of a life lived in the presence of Jesus, through the valleys and mountaintop experiences Sue has had. Any encounter with Sue leaves you imprinted with the understanding that this is a woman who has done the internal work, intertwined her identity resolutely to be found in Christ. As a result, she heals. It is the outflow and byproduct of her being because she herself is a healed woman. Do not simply read the words penned here; allow them to permeate the atmosphere of your soul.*

Wendy Nolasco
General Supervisor
International Church of the Foursquare
Gospel

We want to believe that Jesus is real. We dare to hope in his healing power. Often, we are misled and disappointed. **Held in His Hands** *will not only encourage you with biblical teaching but will cause you to reflect on the power of God in the story of a real-life everyday believer.*

Debbie Alsdorf
Author of Deeper, The Faith Dare, and It's Momplicated

Please read the healing book of Sue, this is wonderful. God has a ministry of healing for Sue. There is a wave of healing flowing across the world. This book of Sue's is going to be instrumental in flaming the healing ministry across the world.

Leslie W. Keegel D.D., D.Min.
Chairman, Global Foursquare Church
President, Church of the Foursquare
Gospel, Sri Lanka

As a current stage 4 cancer patient, it is easy to let the many options and opinions drown out God's quiet whispers. **Held in His Hands** *is a strong reminder that God has a plan for our lives. When we take time to quiet our hearts, we find that God is speaking His Word into our story. We are healed. And Sue reminds us that whether our healing happens here or in heaven, we win. We win because Jesus loves us, and nothing, absolutely nothing, can remove us from His hands.*

Mark and Micki Goodell
Community Pastor and Executive
Assistant, The Highlands Church,
Palmdale, CA

Some of my favorite statements start with 'But God.' There are so many impossibilities we face either physically, emotionally, or relationally, 'But God.' We can have an outcome assigned to us BUT GOD... has other plans, another outcome, a different direction. All for His glory. Sue has shared her real story of 'But God' in her life. Though she was fine with any outcome, God had a plan, and now He had a vessel. To bring the hope of His presence no matter what you are going through and the healing He has for us one way or another.

Mandy Flores
Co-Pastor, The Adventure Church,
Fresno, CA

Held

In His

Hands

A Miracle Story

and

Encouragement for Your Healing

Sue Boldt

Note: The names of everyone mentioned in this book were changed to protect their privacy, except for those who gave me direct permission. For those mentioned, my views on divine healing may not reflect their beliefs.

Table of Contents

Foreword

All of our days...

The circumstances of a believer's life are ordained by God
Oswald Chambers

We all want to believe that Jesus is real. We dare to hope in his healing power. Often, we are misled and disappointed. Still, with everything within us, we want to have courage to continue hoping in the power of God—in the here and now. The book you are holding in your hand will not only encourage you but will cause you to reflect on the power of God in the story of a real-life everyday believer.

There is so much emotion in writing a foreword for this book. I love Sue and have always felt a debt of gratitude for her life and testimony. I am beyond grateful for God's healing hand in her life, but more than that, I am drawn to her balanced and beautiful teaching of God's word. I have watched her transform and grow through the years, and I can honestly tell you, she is the real deal as a Jesus follower.

Looking back, I realize that even before I knew Jesus, God has always been with me. Before I knew him, He knew me. In his grace, I met Sue at the beginning of our Freshmen year in high school. We were young teens, living in a beach town, growing up around influences bigger than us. It was the 70's, the era of sex, drugs, and rock and roll.

Sue, as sweet and fun as she is, became a quick and easy friend. But shortly after we met, she also became friends with Jesus. No longer bringing her teen magazines to the beach, she now brought her marked up paperback bible. I was intrigued but disinterested. After all, all the glory of high school was before us, and I was drawn to the popularity and parties of those years.

Sue continued to follow Jesus, go to church, and lead the Christ on Campus club. She always had a radiating joy that secretly continued to impress me.

I wanted what Sue had. Many times, during those four years, she told me how I too could walk with Jesus. I listened and tucked the information into a corner of my heart, but parties and popularity won out every time. I just didn't have time, space, or courage to follow Jesus. But, by the end of my senior year, I emotionally bottomed out. I was ready, and just before beginning college, I did exactly as Sue had encouraged me, in my bedroom alone, I prayed and began a relationship with Jesus. Since that day in 1973, nothing has ever been the same.

When telling my personal testimony, it always points back to Sue. She was my first point of contact with Christianity and the reason I was drawn to Jesus. The ripple effect of her faith is evidenced in my entire family of origin becoming Christians. As the years have gone by, my life has not been perfect, and neither has Sue's. We both became pastor's wives and had a heart to minister to women. We both have been through mountain tops and deep valleys. In both, God has been with us. We stayed in touch through the years and her life, and faith has made a huge difference in mine. Her friendship and fellowship have been priceless.

I still remember the day that I heard she was in the hospital with a cancer diagnosis. My heart sank. She was vibrant in the faith and was actively reaching women through writing and speaking. Not Sue, Lord, please, not now. In disbelief that this was happening, I hit my knees and poured my heart out to God. I was among many who did the same.

Somehow, I knew that God was not finished with Sue, and perhaps her ministry was just beginning to ramp up. Still, the diagnosis grim. And, though I knew without a doubt that God determines our days, I dared to hope that Sue's limits were not drawing near, but that the limitless love of Christ was going to be glorified through a testimony of healing.

Praise God, that is Sue's incredible story!

Sometimes God heals on earth and other times in heaven. Sue was given more time on earth through the miraculous healing of God's hand. It's not because she is better than anyone or that she has a direct hotline to heaven (though sometimes I believe she does). God is not done with Sue, and she will have meaning and purpose until the day she takes her very last breath—and so will you, and so will I.

> *...the days ordained for me were written in your book*
> *before one of them came to be.*
>
> Psalm 139:16

The book you hold in your hand gives glory to God. It is a personal testimony of Sue's healing as well as a teaching on how to draw near to God yourself. It is beautifully balanced in teaching and intent. It is my prayer that the teaching and testimony in this book will reach many for the glory of God. It is also my prayer that these pages will serve as a teaching resource on healing and experiencing the fullness of God, even when he doesn't heal the way we anticipated. In the end, God is always faithful. He is always at work and He can always be trusted.

I am just one woman, sitting in the stands thanking God for his healing power and cheering my sister Sue on as she courageously shares her story with the world. May God be honored and glorified. And may you, dear reader, be forever changed.

Debbie Alsdorf
Author of Deeper, The Faith Dare, and
It's Momplicated

Forward

Introduction

Just last evening, I received an email from my oncologist from the University of California, Los Angeles (UCLA). It was a simple message that caused me to drop to my knees in thanksgiving and made my eyes well up with grateful tears, once again. The message read:

CT scans look very good

No more, no less. Not even any punctuation. That message stated what has been called a continuing miracle by the medical community—my healing from stage 4 incurable non-functioning adrenocortical carcinoma.

I pray the little book you hold in your hands will encourage your heart and cause you to seek God's power for your health journey. Possibly, it isn't you who has a difficult diagnosis, but a loved one. If that is the case, I hope that you will find strength, comfort, peace, and even joy. I desire most of all, that whatever your situation, you would know in the depths of your heart, no matter your life's story, God loves you. He really, really, really does.

This book has two sections. The first is the story of my healing journey of faith when diagnosed with terminal, incurable cancer some years ago. Although there is much to write about God's faithfulness to me, I have only noted what I thought might be meaningful.

In the second section of *Held in His Hands*, I attempt to give some practical help in areas of walking with the Lord Jesus that have been so beneficial to me both now, and when facing cancer. Namely, how to invite Him into your own life and situation; the power of His written Word, the Bible; cultivating a quiet time in our fast-paced world; and recognizing the power of the third Person of the Trinity, the Holy Spirit. I also have interspersed some thoughts that have come to me as Jesus walked me down the path to healing.

I have had the privilege of sitting under the best pastoral care and teaching a person could have with Jim Hayford, Ralph Moore, Daniel Brown, Ph.D., and my husband, Randy. The teachings and writings of Jack Hayford, Litt.D., have also inspired me much and taught me well.

Instead of being goofy, stubborn, or flat-out weird, I have been scripturally taught to *contend for the authentic* concerning God's work in a human life on every level. However, to keep this book simple and to the point, you *will not* find in-depth doctrine or theology about what God's Word has to say about physical healing. A small list of other Biblical study books about physical healing is provided if you care to do further inquiry.

God still works healing miracles today. Nevertheless, how He does it is up to Him. And yet, there are more vital and crucial gifts He wants to give each of us. Gifts of extraordinary joy and grace in adversity, supernatural strength and courage in the middle of despair, and His unlimited power to be more than a conqueror in any situation. So, let's keep our eyes, minds, and hearts on the Giver of all gifts, the Lord Jesus Christ. Because when we do, we will always have everything we need or could ever hope for.

Love in Him,

Sue

Part One

My Story

1

Cabin Retreat

He who dwells in the secret place
of the Most High
Shall abide under the shadow of the Almighty.

Psalm 91:1

It all began as time away on a personal retreat in October of 2008. As a longtime believer in Jesus, I headed to our family cabin for a weekend to lean hard into His presence. I was seeking to be refreshed, renewed, and to hear from God's heart to mine as I flew from Sacramento to Southern California, rented a car, and drove to Big Bear Lake. I looked forward to this reprieve from my full-time work at a large hospital in the same San Francisco Bay Area city where my husband, Randy, and I were pastors of a growing young church.

On Saturday morning, as I knelt on the old carpeting of the cabin floor with my Bible and journal, I profoundly experienced the Lord's presence. By that, I mean, an almost indescribable warmth inside me, like a soothing oil, laced with a deep sense of well-being. Soon into my quiet time, I opened my Bible to some well-worn passages from the old prophet, Isaiah, chapters 40-45. The Holy Spirit spoke to my heart through many of the words, but as I arrived in Chapter 41, I sensed He was emphasizing verses 10-13:

> *Fear not, for I am with you;*
> *Be not dismayed, for I am your God.*
> *I will strengthen you,*

Yes, I will help you,
I will uphold you with My righteous right hand.

Behold, all those who were incensed against you
Shall be ashamed and disgraced;
They shall be as nothing,
And those who strive with you shall perish.

You shall seek them and not find them—
Those who contended with you.
Those who war against you
Shall be as nothing,
As a nonexistent thing.

For I, the LORD your God, will hold your right hand,
Saying to you, 'Fear not, I will help you.

Isaiah 41:10-13

I had a soft impression upon my heart and mind, the subtle voice of the Holy Spirit, telling me that something was coming my way, but I was *not to be afraid*. He would hold me with His right hand and cause my enemy to be as *a non-existent thing*. I didn't have any specifics, but I surmised that some disruption might occur in our church that was starting to grow, or in my ministry, which seemed to be taking off a little bit. Regardless of this news, I felt overwhelming joy. I knew I wasn't going to be afraid of what happened, and I did not experience any fear at that moment. His words to me—from His Word—did not carry any sense of dread or foreboding like one might think a premonition would. Instead, the Bible verses came with a sense of blessing and hope.

A few days later, upon my return home, I had another significant time with the Lord Jesus. As was my custom after work, I walked our large dog to the beautiful grounds of the decommissioned naval chapel near our home on Mare Island, in Vallejo. I had my Bible and journal, and I was having a great quiet time with God, relaxing with my furry friend after a busy day's work. Once again, I significantly experienced the Lord's presence. As I looked up into the eucalyptus trees surrounding the chapel, I saw multitudes of monarch butterflies! It seemed like a lovely gift from the Lord sent special delivery to me. I remember getting a little teary with happiness, but honestly, not thinking it meant anything other than a sweet gift of beauty from the hand of a marvelous Creator.

I will pause here to say that throughout my healing journey, there were countless incidents where I felt a deep resonance in my heart that God was encouraging me. He used circumstances through nature, situations I found myself in, or divine, unexpected appointments with people reiterating that He was with me. Countless times, while reading His Word, I felt a deep confirmation in my heart that a passage of Scripture was speaking *life* to me. The same was true when I might get a phrase or a picture in my mind that would bring strength as it confirmed what He had spoken to me out of Isaiah 41. Suffice to say, I cannot recount them all, and I will only share a few of them here in the hope that you will be encouraged too.

A Morning to Remember…

The week we were to leave for Taiwan on a mission trip, I woke up a few hours after midnight on Sunday morning with severe abdominal pain on my right side. I prayed for a little bit, took a few tablets of ibuprofen, but the pain would not subside. When matters worsened, I woke Randy up to pray for me, nevertheless, the pain kept gradually escalating. We called the advice department at the hospital where I worked, and after a battery of questions, the attending physician told me to come to the Emergency Department (ED). As Randy and I drove across the bridge that connected our Mare Island home to the mainland of Vallejo, I profoundly recognized the Lord's nearness, even in the mounting pain. I then realized that I was facing the trial the Lord had spoken to me about a few weeks before.

When Randy and I entered the ED, the children's ministry supervisor from our church and a registered nurse, Sheila Alfonso, unexpectedly greeted us. Due to an unforeseen shift change, Sheila *just happened to be* the triage RN that early morning! Sheila admitted me quickly into that hopping, Saturday night-Sunday-morning ED, where I was taken for an immediate CT scan[1] to look for the likely culprit of my pain—an appendix issue or a kidney stone.

The pain increased, and no amount of medication brought relief, but a confident and overflowing joy in my heart kept growing as well. The same joy that I had felt at the cabin was pouring into me once again as I prayed silently and quietly in my spiritual language.[2] And, thinking my ordeal would be over quickly, I encouraged Randy to head to the church building to lead the church services that morning.

After several hours, the right-side abdominal pain was still excruciating. I'd had three natural births with our children that seemed like a cakewalk compared to this! Once again, the ED staff wheeled me into the radiology department for a CT scan, and with Randy by my side, the attending ED physician informed us that I had a large abdominal mass, about the size of a football, 17cm x 20cm. The two CT scans revealed that the tumor, which appeared to be attached to one of my adrenal glands, had ruptured. Immediate surgery was required to stop the internal bleeding and remove the mass. The ED doctor had rousted three surgeons from watching their televised Sunday afternoon football games: a urologist, a cardiologist, and a surgeon who specialized in abdominal surgery.

It seemed preposterous that I had not known I had a tumor that large! I wear a smallish size, however, the mass was flat and hadn't caused my tummy to protrude. Instead, my waistline had seemed a little thicker to me, which I had previously chalked up to passing the fifty-year mark in age. Later, when I had the opportunity to view one of these CT scans with a radiologist from our church, he pointed out that all of my organs had moved into different locations from where they should be because of the mass's growth. The tumor was also wrapping around my vena cava, the largest vein in the human body, transporting blood from the abdomen to the right side of the heart. I went into emergency surgery to save my life, later learning that my prospects for surviving the operation had been slim to none.

It took the surgeons and their team an hour and a half to staunch a pool of blood in my abdomen that would not stop hemorrhaging because my platelets were low, and my blood was unable to clot. I received an almost complete transfusion.

With a total of five and one-half hours on the operating table, I made it through. The surgeons had cut me in two and removed one of my adrenal glands, and the cardiologist had severed my vena cava artery to release the grip of the mass and sewn it back together. The surgeons were hopeful that they had captured and removed the mass that was in pieces. Nevertheless, we would have to wait for a final pathology report to see if the tumor was malignant.

I had total peace. I had joy unspeakable. Friends jokingly commented that my happiness was possibly the result of all the post-surgery morphine prescribed! But no, this was the joy and peace of Jesus that the Bible calls beyond human comprehension.[3] Although I couldn't stand up, my vision was blurry, and I would not be able to eat or drink for a week, the surgery was deemed a success. Randy was constantly with me, and our adult daughters, Dayspring and Shiloh, came to be with us. The next day, my story was apparently the talk of the ED department due to the size of the mass and the extensive surgery.

Immediately, as I recuperated in the med-surg wing of the hospital for the next seven days, I started receiving flower bouquets, and by the end of the week's stay, there were almost twenty bouquets. In maybe not the best bedside manner, one nurse remarked that my room looked like a funeral parlor!

One of the first bouquets I received came from the team I worked with at the hospital. It was a huge bouquet full of fall colors and tucked within the arrangement was a *silk monarch butterfly*. I couldn't believe it. Just a week earlier, the Lord had met me on the Mare Island Chapel grounds with a lavish gift of monarch butterflies. I thought of this as a divine coincidence; God was saying He was with me, and I was not to be afraid. My enemy, whatever it was, would be as a non-existent thing!

On the second day after the surgery, longtime friends, Pastors Foch and

Debbie Fuller came to pray for me, bringing with them a couple who *happened* to be visiting them. Dr. Leslie and Belen Keegel, Sri Lankan pastors and evangelists, are well-known and respected in the worldwide Christian community. Leslie is well acquainted with the Holy Spirit's gift of physical healing. Together, the Keegels and Fullers listened to my bedside story as I shared my cabin encounter with the Lord, the verses from Isaiah, the butterflies in the park, and the butterfly bouquet. I sounded a bit crazy, even to myself! It was the first time I remember weeping a tad as I spoke to them. *Am I nuts to think the Lord spoke to me out of Isaiah 41? The butterflies, are they just wishful thinking?*

I remember Leslie stepping forward, closer to my bed, where I had every conceivable piece of medical apparatus attached to me. He told me that although he couldn't back up his words doctrinally, he sensed the Holy Spirit telling him that I needed to go through this experience, and it was for my ministry. He explained that sometimes those who will be used by the Lord Jesus to minister healing must go through the valley of trial themselves to become a vessel He can use. He also had a Scripture for me:

> *There is no one like the God of Jeshurun,*
> *Who rides the heavens to help you,*
> *And in His excellency on the clouds.*
>
> *The eternal God is your refuge,*
> *And underneath are the everlasting arms;*
> *He will thrust out the enemy from before you,*
> *And will say, 'Destroy!'*
>
> *Then Israel shall dwell in safety,*
> *The fountain of Jacob alone,*
> *In a land of grain and new wine;*
> *His heavens shall also drop dew.*
>
> *Happy are you, O Israel!*
> *Who is like you, a people saved by the LORD,*
> *The shield of your help*
> *And the sword of your majesty!*

Your enemies shall submit to you,
And you shall tread down their high places.

Deuteronomy 33:26-29

The two couples then prayed for me.

Later that afternoon, Dayspring came back to the hospital. *Mom!* She handprinted out an online article about butterflies:

> *The butterfly finally emerges from the now transparent*
> *chrysalis. It inflates its wings with a pool of blood it has*
> *stored in its abdomen. When this is done, the monarch*
> *expels any excess fluid and rests. The butterfly waits until*
> *its wings stiffen and dry before it flies away to start the*
> *cycle of life all over again.4*

Dayspring and I both had the same line of thought. The surgeons had emphasized to our family how deadly the pool of blood in my abdomen had been. Here, the correlation with the monarch butterfly struck our hearts that God was in the details. From nearly dying, my ministry would begin to take flight through my testimony of what He was working in my life.

Yes, it may be a stretch to think this way, nevertheless, this portion of my story has deeply moved countless listeners. They are encouraged to know how intimately and intentionally God wants to daily speak into *each* of our lives. How often have I missed His cues because I was so wrapped up in my way of doing things–the busyness of life, not even asking to see His hand at work? You, too? Possibly it takes a significant event to open our eyes and ears to begin to see that God is always talking and pursuing us.

Dayspring had something else to share. She had read a few verses further in Isaiah 41:

> *"Fear not, you worm Jacob,*
> *You men of Israel!*

I will help you," says the LORD
And your Redeemer, the Holy One of Israel.

"Behold, I will make you into a new threshing sledge
with sharp teeth;

You shall thresh the mountains and beat them small,
And make the hills like chaff."

Isaiah 41:14-15

My daughter and I both read from the same study Bible version. Dayspring pointed out to me the study Bible's note for verse 14:

Israel is called a worm. A symbol of weakness, but Yahweh will make His servant into a threshing sledge, an instrument that in His hands will pulverize the mountains, her current difficulties. The verses are a call to expect deliverance as the people rejoice in the Lord.[5]

These words spoke directly to me and they continue to do so today. From God's Word, I recognize that as a believer in Jesus, He has given you and me authority in His Name to bring down any of Satan's attacks or weaponry against us. Although we are genuinely weak–I love the reference to being a worm–we are positioned in God's strength to topple the mountains in our lives, the lives of others, and wherever or for whatever He calls us to do battle to bring the reign of His kingdom.

At the end of the week in the hospital, a young urologist came to check on me in place of my original surgeon who was on his day off from work. At first, the young doctor was happy and upbeat, talkative, and positive. He left the room for a few minutes, but then returned. This time, his head hung low, and he talked to me quietly. In those short minutes, the pathology report had come in. The diagnosis: *Non-functioning Adrenocortical Carcinoma.*

The diagnosis was pretty much a death sentence.

The urologist told me it was an extremely aggressive cancer, and due to my age and the enormous size of the tumor, I had less than a 10% chance of surviving to five years. The cancer's disturbing characteristics were its ability to work in stealth mode, and when discovered, it was usually too late for recovery. The second issue with the disease was its tendency to reoccur until it took the patient's life. The cancer was also so rare that a physician might only see one patient with this diagnosis in their lifetime.

The physician and I talked about what I should expect next when meeting with an oncologist. The man looked so sad, I finally said to him, *It's okay Dr. Henry, I am not afraid to die.* I truly meant what I said. It was just a quiet, but genuine declaration. He then lifted his head for the first time since walking into the room and stated, *It's people like you who make it.*

Next Steps...

I soon learned that there was no known cure for this type of cancer and that regular chemotherapy infusion was ineffective. The only treatment advised for adrenocortical carcinoma was a highly toxic *oral* chemotherapy called *Mitotane.* This drug is a derivative of the insecticide DDT, that is taken daily, throughout the day, based on a dosage that a patient could tolerate. It would be up to me to decide if I wanted to risk taking this medication that might kill me before the cancer did! The only trial study of Mitotane had taken place in Europe with 177 patients over twenty years.[6] The test results were dismal. Mitotane was not a cure, but it might extend my life by a few months.

There is something so sweet about the presence of God when in a weakened state. His grace *is more than enough,* just as the apostle Paul tells us in 2 Corinthians 12:7-10. I was released from the hospital, barely able to stand or walk, but with a profound, physical experience of the warmth and joyful, sweet, and powerful sense of the Holy Spirit within my being. An abiding knowledge, not only in my thoughts, but in my heart, that Jesus was holding me with His right hand.

Our family, friends, and church rallied to support us in prayer, providing food, cleaning our home, walking the dog, and anything else we needed.

Many had Bible verses to give me that confirmed that Jesus held me tight. I seemed to be in almost constant communion with the Lord, and the overwhelming presence of His love made being worried or anxious impossible. Fear just didn't happen. I continually read God's Word, always coming back to: *do not be afraid, I hold you with my right hand; your enemy shall be as a non-existent thing!*

I only remember a few times, just before getting into bed at night, when a sense of dread would begin to sweep over me. I told Randy that I needed to go downstairs and spend time with Jesus to stop this onslaught, and each time, God met me there. The anxiety would lift, and I could sleep peacefully. My years of learning that God's presence is the quickest, most cost-effective, and the best cure for an anxiety attack were all put into play in those moments. *His perfect love does cast out fear.*[7]

My first CT scan after surgery was clear of any sight of further cancerous lesions! Oh, how we rejoiced that the enemy was searched for but not found.[8]

Randy and I took a few weeks to seek the Lord about my taking Mitotane, and we both sensed His leading to begin the treatment. I was started on a low dosage of it with incremental increases to see what I could tolerate along with the hormone, cortisol, that Mitotane suppressed in my body. I went back to work after twelve weeks, having just started the medication.

I have since talked to a woman who had the same adrenal cancer and was prescribed the same dosage of Mitotane as me. She was completely bedridden and passed away within a few months of our initial contact. On the other hand, I was able to return to a new position within the healthcare company I worked for at a newly built hospital. I often walked the length of the new building and daily climbed the four flights of stairs to build my stamina.

My oncologist and endocrinologist required constant lab work to monitor my treatment, however, after eighteen months of the medication, when my skin blackened, my balance became unsteady, and my quality of life began to deteriorate, Randy and I believed that it was time to taper off the Mitotane.

We had both doctors' blessings to discontinue it. They again expressed that there was no hard evidence that the chemo medication wasn't doing more harm than good because I had no visible cancer lesions each time I was screened.

None of my attending physicians could believe that I was cancer-free! Mine was a case study observed by many doctors in the vast healthcare organization where I was employed. I have since been introduced to three adrenal cancer patients across the United States, and none of them survived past a few months of my meeting them.

But God. Those wonderful two words spoken throughout the Bible when God intervenes in human affairs. He kept giving me verses from the Scriptures to encourage me, and others also had Bible verses, words, and pictures in their hearts and minds to strengthen me. I kept having sweet love notes from the Lord in the craziest ways, always reminding me that He held me by His mighty hand. Daily life with its highs and lows ensued, but His joy within me never waned, as both Randy and I experienced much growth and blessing in our ministries.

Chapter 1

2

Once Again

Behold, I will make you
into a new threshing sledge...
You shall thresh the mountains and beat them small,
And... the wind shall carry them away...
You shall rejoice in the LORD,
And glory in the Holy One of Israel.

Isaiah 41:15-16

Three and a half years later, a routine CT scan revealed that the cancer had returned. My oncologist told us that I officially had Stage 4 incurable cancer.

The pronouncement of cancer, once again, caused both Randy and me to pause and immediately get on our faces before God. There is nothing quite like faceplant-in-the-carpet time. I never demanded that God heal me, and I never believed He owed me anything, but we needed to hear what He would say to us now.

We believe the truth that physical healing is available to a Christian believer based on Christ's work on the cross:

> *But He was wounded for our transgressions,*
> *He was bruised for our iniquities;*
> *The chastisement for our peace was upon Him,*
> *And by His stripes we are healed.*

Isaiah 53:5

This verse is repeated in the Gospel of *Matthew 8:16-17*, describing Jesus' physical healing ministry as he walked the earth, and once again, by Peter, in *1 Peter 2:24*. Nevertheless, through our years of ministry, we came to recognize a fine line between faith in Him and His promises, and faith in our faith and our strong will to try and make something happen.

God has given us His Word to guide, lead, teach, correct, encourage, strengthen, and equip us for spiritual battles. However, when Randy and I were much younger, we erred by trying to *use* God's Word to claim whatever *we* asked for. Again, it is a fine line of being led by the Holy Spirit or acting upon the whim of our flesh. During this thankfully short season of our lives, we often negated hearing from the Holy Spirit or taking our God-given responsibility about a situation.

For instance, if we had financial woes, all we had to do was claim more money in our checking account, according to *Philippians 4:19*. Never mind that we might actually have to go get a job to cover our expenses!

During this time, if we took medicine, saw a doctor, or received medical care, we considered this to be a lack of faith, nullifying the Word of God for healing. Living this way nearly shipwrecked our lives. When the emphasis became more about what we did or didn't do, or our faith or lack of it, rather than loving and trusting God, our belief system became toxic. The pursuit of the gift of things or healing had taken preeminence over the pursuit of the Giver alone, the Lord Jesus.

To this day, both Randy and I believe that physical healing is part of the atoning work of Jesus. Yet, at the same time, the Lord, in His infinite love and mercy, works through science to reveal how He made our physical bodies work and how they can be fixed. Today, I believe Jesus works congruently in the miraculous along with the medical. It is up to each individual to have a personal (notice, I didn't say perfect!) walk with God to be led to the course of action they should or shouldn't take when it comes to physical, mental, or emotional healing. The Lord still works miracles outside medicine or natural laws, but I don't believe that medicine nullifies the miraculous or that the miraculous only takes place outside of medicine.

The big question for someone to ask themselves in any situation, whether it is an illness or any other calamity, is *who or what am I trusting?* Am I running to medicine before I even consult with the Lord about what to do? Or am I blindly saying that God only works one way and that cuts off any other avenues of help He may be providing? Even when Jesus ministered miracle healing to the multitudes, He used a variety of methods by the leading of the Holy Spirit.[1]

One size does not fit all situations, and this is the exciting life of the Christian—being led by the Holy Spirit in every situation. It is also the thrill of the power of God's Word when it is ignited by the Holy Spirit, affecting what we say and do and what happens. You can move forward confidently when you are sure you have heard His course of action to take, whatever route it might be.

King Asa of Judah exemplifies the mistake of taking matters in his own hands and not drawing near to God to hear what He might say for his physical healing. Even after the prophet Hanani had encouraged Asa's faith prior to his illness by saying, *The eyes of the Lord search the whole earth, to show Himself strong on behalf of those whose heart is loyal to Him,* the Bible records that Asa did not seek the Lord. Instead, he *only* consulted with physicians, which resulted in his death.[2]

When the cancer returned, both Randy and I went back into a place of quiet with Jesus. From there, He confirmed to us that His original word out of *Isaiah 41:10-13,* had not changed, and I kept receiving assurance from the Holy Spirit that I was going to be okay, even healed.

Once again, something out of the ordinary would happen daily, confirming that the Lord held me close and that I was not to be afraid. What an incredible blessing to walk into my workplace each morning feeling covered and protected where I had many opportunities to pray for staff members and patients that entered my office. My workplace Bible study was a huge blessing and encouragement to me, along with the growth numerically and spiritually in our church.

Moving Forward...

My oncologist referred me to a different region in the healthcare organization for my second surgery. There, Dr. Liu, who specialized in abdominal tumors, would lead the surgical team.

We had an interesting first meeting with Dr. Liu, who was Taiwanese. Because Randy and I traveled twice a year to Taiwan to teach for the gospel mission organization, Youth With a Mission (YWAM), Dr. Liu wanted to learn about our faith and what we did in Taiwan. One of his medical assistants even had a *Nothing is Impossible with God* sign on her cabinet, but he seemed unsure of what having faith meant. And, though my oncologist seemed hopeful for my outcome after surgery because the mass was small and localized, Dr. Liu didn't paint as pretty a picture. He warned me that I might lose a kidney.

Both Randy and I were sobered after leaving his office. It is in those times that eternity feels a breath away, and you either make a choice to run towards the Lord Jesus or run from Him, and we decided to run toward Him.

I felt led by the Holy Spirit to set aside a Saturday for fasting and prayer. In the late afternoon, in the front room of our home, where I frequently went to meet with Jesus, these verses were highlighted in my heart:

> *Nevertheless, I will bring health and healing to it; I will heal my people and will let them enjoy abundant peace and security. ...*
>
> *Then this city will bring me renown, joy, praise and honor before all nations on earth that hear of all the good things I do for it; and they will be in awe and will tremble at the abundant prosperity and peace I provide for it.'...*
>
> *'The days are coming,' declares the LORD, 'when I will*

fulfill the good promise I made to the people of Israel and Judah.'

Jeremiah 33:6, 9, 14 NIV

With my Greek-Hebrew study Bible, I looked up the original Hebrew wording for *health* in verse six. The word means *to make long, live long, healing, health, with the sense of restoring to soundness.*[3] My heart and mind were comforted by this promise from God's Word directly to me.

I spoke at a women's retreat in Wisconsin right before the scheduled surgery in March of 2012. It was here in the middle of this winter wonderland that the Lord drew me to a deeper place of surrender than I have ever known, taking place after the Saturday night meeting when I was alone in my room. As I lay in bed, I pondered the possibility that the Lord's healing word might actually mean that He would heal me in heaven, where all sickness and suffering will cease. Honestly, these thoughts had been on my mind for a few days.

Tears came for how I would miss Randy, our kids, and grandkids. I wasn't sobbing, but just those quiet tears that fall when you feel a deep longing or heartache. In that still moment in the middle of the night, the Lord told me that *I wasn't to prepare to die*. In other words, He called me to surrender *all my thoughts* about the future and trust Him. Hearing this was profound for me and acting upon His directive brought unexplainable peace and comfort. He was calling me to a deeper surrender of my life in the context of my thinking.

The next morning was the final session of the retreat where we had a marvelous time praising God because of all the amazing things He had done the entire weekend. The worship band concluded, but as the worship leader was leaving the stage, before I would come up to share one last time, she abruptly walked back to her microphone. She then literally yelled to the audience of women, *Be healed and live long!* It was the exact wording of the *Jeremiah 33:6* definition that I had read right before the retreat. I sensed the Lord was blessing my fresh surrender to Him from the night before.

Before the retreat ended, about 150 women surrounded me and prayed for me. One woman had a picture in her mind that Jesus was standing in front of me, reaching into my abdomen and directly taking the small mass out from my body. I knew this meant the surgery would go well and Jesus would take the cancer.

Our daughter, Shiloh, and her family came to visit the Sunday before surgery to enjoy some good old-fashioned fun before I would be sidelined in recovery. While her kids and I climbed the jungle gym on the local school playground, I noticed a tiny gold ring almost buried in the sawdust. Yes, a small, child-sized ring with minuscule diamonds forming a cross on top of it. I called the school the next day and inquired if anyone had been looking for the missing ring. *No*, was the answer, and they took my name and phone number in case anyone came looking. I have the ring to this day, and I have worn it constantly on my right-hand little finger. A gift, once again, out of many such incidents, where Lord Jesus demonstrated His nearness and care for me.

With Dr. Liu, a new surgical team, and a new hospital for me, my second procedure took place in April 2012. For this surgery, I had the joy of our son, Jeremy, taking turns with Randy to stay with me in the hospital. Although a small portion of one lung was resected, I did not lose a kidney. My oncologist recommended that I start taking Mitotane again, and after prayer, I once again began a low dose of the medication.

Two significant events impacted my life within a few months after the second surgery. A longtime friend was diagnosed with cancer, and another close friend died suddenly.

I had known Jenna for years, having gone through ministry school together with our husbands. Her family's move to another state and then to work with a mission organization in Mozambique caused our visits to be very infrequent, but we kept in touch. Jenna and her husband had moved back to the San Francisco Bay Area where she had been diagnosed with ovarian cancer and had surgery to remove the cancerous mass. Her oncologist–from the same healthcare company I worked for—had recommended that she have infusion chemotherapy and radiation according to treatment protocols.

Jenna came out to our church for prayer, and we met for lunch soon after. She was overflowing with enthusiasm for the natural, alternative treatment she was following, instead of following her physician's directions. We talked at great length about slowing down our lives entirely and resting continuously. Jenna had a larger-than-life personality that people adored; nevertheless, after spending time with her, I was shaken. I wondered if I was on the wrong road. Should I follow her path to healing?

It was face-down-in-the-carpet time again with the Lord and His Word. What was *He* telling me?

The Holy Spirit reminded me again of the many Scripture passages He had given me, and the course I was taking. Instead of slowing down, I continued to work full-time, lead a thriving women's ministry at our church, take care of my elderly dad from a distance, and speak at women's events.

About a year later, in the few months leading up to Jenna's passing through heaven's doors, she told me that she realized how much *in control* she had been by choosing *how* her healing would come. When she sought chemotherapy, it was too late. It wasn't that her methods for obtaining health and healing were wrong, but Jenna recognized *her insistence* about how it would come had blinded her. Jenna then experienced peace and joy as she renewed fresh surrender to Him in the final days and weeks of her life.

In early November, the same year as my second surgery, and just after meeting with Jenna, we learned that our longtime friend, Don Gillman had abruptly passed into the Lord's presence due to a brain aneurism while on a daily run. Randy and I had just returned home from a mission trip to Taiwan, where Don was the Youth With a Mission (YWAM) base leader, the national leader for the organization in Taiwan, and their East Asia Director for Frontier Missions.

Don lived under an anointing and call of a modern-day apostle with a global view to reach the world with the gospel. His non-stop travels, teaching, and evangelizing in some of the world's most unreached, and frankly scariest, nations for the gospel, had impacted countless multitudes in every region of the globe. His life also influenced thousands of young believers to the mission field or full-time service for Jesus.

I had once thought that Don did too much. And maybe at times, that was true, but the fact was that he lived on assignment for God and loved every minute of it. His passing spoke volumes to me. The day we learned of his homegoing, I made a conscious decision that whatever time I had left on this planet, I would live it in hot pursuit of the work of the Holy Spirit in my life to impact my world.

3

Held in His Hands

For I, the LORD your God,
will hold your right hand,
Saying to you,
'Fear not, I will help you.'

Isaiah 41:13

Three days after finding out about Don's passing, I learned that the adrenocortical cancer had returned for a third time according to my recent CT scan. It had only been seven months since my second surgery

My oncologist broke the news to me over the phone in the middle of a busy workday just as I was about to break for lunch with the Bible study group I led. He told me that because the cancer had returned so shortly after its last appearance, and because it appeared to have metastasized to my liver, I was *winding down*. He said I was dying. He instructed me to get my affairs in order. I needed to prepare an Advance Directive–a legal document that specifies what actions should be taken for my health for when I would be unable to make those decisions on my own. He advised me to not have any more CT scans, and he was referring me to the palliative care department and that someone would be contacting me in the next few days.

But what about surgery? I asked. He didn't advise it. It was time to accept that this cancer was incurable and deal with it.

But what about continuing to have CT scans so that I could track the cancer's growth? No, what would be the point of knowing?

I remembered Dr. Liu, my surgeon, telling me that he had performed returning cancer operations in the past, and I asked if I could talk to Dr. Liu directly. My doctor didn't think that was a good idea, but he couldn't stop me from asking. I called Randy, and we prayed together on the phone.

Truthfully, I was emotionally shaken. But, then and there, after my oncologist's dire phone call, I decided to live like our friend Don had, full-out for Jesus as best I could as long as the Holy Spirit would empower me. I would continue to go, teach, and preach until I couldn't go anymore. What a relief to make that decision as I headed into my Bible study with fresh purpose.

When Randy and I pursued our Savior that night, we both sensed that He tightly held us both. Oh, how I thank God for my husband who constantly stood beside me. I don't know what is more challenging, receiving a difficult diagnosis for yourself, or watching a beloved one go through an illness. Both participants carry a load that only God can bear. Praying separately and together, we felt peace about reaching out to Dr. Liu. If he was willing to operate, the surgery might buy me a few more months to see what the Lord might do for me.

The next day, I consulted with the physician in chief at the large clinic where I now worked. I served Dr. Walters as her administrative assistant, considering her to be not only my boss and my primary care physician, but also a dear friend. She went to bat for me with the oncology department's head doctor about overriding their decision regarding no surgery. However, the oncology head supported the staff doctor's no treatment plan and that a second opinion was not necessary.

Dr. Walters then agreed with my decision to contact Dr. Liu, my second surgeon, for his opinion and to see if he would be willing to operate to debulk the new tumor. Reaching out to Dr. Liu meant abandoning my current oncologist and being reassigned to the region of my healthcare company where Dr. Liu practiced.

Dr. Liu was willing to look at my most recent CT scan. He then ordered an additional PET scan[1] that verified the cancer had indeed returned.

Nevertheless, he agreed to do the surgery because, in spite of the cancer, I was completely healthy! However, he was in no rush to perform the operation, and it was scheduled in late February, about three months away.

Randy and I made a very personal decision *not* to call everyone we knew to pray for me, although many had never stopped! Only our children and a small group of people from our church knew about the cancer's return. It was not that we believed people's prayers didn't matter, but for me, this third time around, both Randy and I needed to stay in tune with what the Lord was speaking to us without any distraction. I felt surrounded with the comfort and happiness of His presence, and I had peace. Christmas came and went with our family, and it was a memorable and meaningful time.

A few weeks before surgery, I spoke at a women's event for a church in Sacramento, where I shared on Saturday, and Randy preached for their Sunday morning service. On the drive home, Randy commented to me that the Lord never promised to remove the cancer from my body, but His word was that it would be *as a non-existent thing*.[2] That moment, we both just knew I was going to live. It didn't matter if the cancer had metastasized–I was going to be okay. And the reason it didn't matter if it was there or not, was because it was powerless over me. In the moment that Randy spoke those words, I believe we received a Holy Spirit gift of faith, a faith completely beyond our natural beliefs.[3] It just was. We just knew. It was a done deal that I would live.

A Healing Day...

On the day of surgery, Dr. Liu came to the room as I was being prepped for the operation, and he gently told me I was dying. He had consulted with other physicians regarding my case about blasting me with radiation while I was still in surgery, yet, everyone he talked to agreed that it was the end for me, and radiation would not help. Dr. Liu promised to be aggressive about removing the cancer he found even though he said I was *winding down.*

The Holy Spirit covered me in comfort as I was wheeled into the operating theater to meet the second surgeon who would be assisting the procedure and the rest of the surgical team.

Well into the surgery, Dr. Liu came out to talk to Randy. Taking him into a smaller office, Dr. Liu began speaking with a pained expression on his face. The surgeon said, *Randy, I know people are praying for Sue; please tell them to keep it up. I haven't fully finished the operation yet, but I have been sending sections of her liver, lung, diaphragm, tissue surrounding her kidney, and in another area to the pathology department.* **We cannot find any cancer!** *There are no traces of any lesions. We will need to get the final pathology report in a few days,* **but we can't find any cancer anywhere!**

I still had hours of recovery before Randy could tell me the news through his joyful tears. What can I say? We were rejoicing and rejoicing! I still had to recover from major surgery, and I remained in the hospital for a week, but nothing could quench the jubilation and sense of wonder Randy and I experienced in Christ. What took place was what He had promised—*my enemy was a non-existent thing.*

Dr. Liu came to visit me when I awoke, and as Randy described, he looked pained, explaining that I had no apparent need for the surgery—yet I did! We needed confirmation that God had done a *miracle*, the very word Dr. Liu used to describe what happened to me.

During my week-long hospital stay, I was transferred to Room 316—yes, think about the Bible passage…

> *For God so loved the world that He gave His only begotten Son, that whoever believes in Him should not perish but have everlasting life.*

> John 3:16

In Room 316, a nurse attended me that had been my nurse while recuperating from the second surgery. We both remembered each other, although ten months had passed. She had told me the year before, and she repeated to me again, that her brothers in Saudi Arabia had become Christians. She shared that they were continually praying for her to respond to the gospel, and now, the news that I was cancer-free had deeply moved her heart. Before I left the hospital, I had the great privilege of leading her to Christ, giving her a Bible, and finding her a vibrant church located on the street where she lived.

The final pathology report came to my email after arriving home. The official documentation–which I have kept–confirmed the surgery results. There was no cancer in any of the five tissue resections taken for examination. My new oncologist recommended I *stop* taking the chemotherapy medication, Mitotane, because of its toxicity and the cancer had returned with its use anyway. Five years later, after having continually clear CT scans, my oncologist and I agreed that having stopped the medication had been a good decision.

Now, in retirement from my healthcare employment and from being senior pastors, Randy and I have moved to southern California. I have new healthcare providers with the University of California, Los Angeles. My new UCLA oncologist and endocrinologist are incredulous at my medical charts. They concur that there is no explanation for my good health but a miraculous touch from God's loving hand.

I have since lived lavishly and well. Teaching the power of the Holy Spirit and God's Word continues through our lives on every level and my cancer healing is only a small portion of what I share when asked to speak or minister. Randy will often say that my testimony's power rests upon the felt and genuine joy, comfort, and hope of what we experienced, rather than the healing itself.

I continue to have regular CT scans and I still hold my life loosely, placing it entirely in Jesus' hands. He has the final say, and I find great comfort in this truth. I pray that you will experience the thrill of His comfort, joy, strength, and healing, too.

Part Two

Encouragement
for
Healing

4

Inviting Him In

The LORD has appeared of old to me, saying:
"Yes, I have loved you with an everlasting love;
Therefore with lovingkindness
I have drawn you."

Jeremiah 31:3

Let's begin this section with one of the most profound truths of the Bible.

The Lord God Almighty who created heaven and earth, and intimately created you, loves you beyond reason. His love relentlessly pursues you all the days of your life.[1]

Hearing these words may be difficult as you face a diagnosis that you do not want, or simply when you listen to the latest news report about world events.

Where is God in all this tragedy?

The Bible tells us that God created the world as we know it with a passion for beauty, health, fellowship, fulness, purpose, satisfaction, and life. He created man and woman in His likeness, with the intention of deep and loving communion with them. Nevertheless, when a fallen angel from heaven, the devil,[2] deceived the man and woman into thinking that God was holding out on them, they ate from the only tree God had forbidden them to partake of in the Garden of Eden.[3]

The couple's bite from the tree of the knowledge of good and evil unleashed several tragic circumstances that the Lord had warned them would take place if they didn't listen to His one command. In their disobedience…

- They ushered in evil, rupturing the pristine and flawless world God had created with death, disaster, disease, selfishness, sin, and pain.[4]

- The *spirit* within the man and woman—which is the unseen, eternal place within the human life where perfect union with the Godhead is enjoyed—no longer had the Holy Spirit's life-breath.[5] Meaning that Adam and Eve spiritually died, passing that same death to all people. Yes, you and me.[6]

- Adam and Eve lost the dominion and rule over the earth, which the Father, Son, and Holy Spirit had given them. In truth, they handed over their authority to the serpent—the devil—who had deceived them.[7]

- Their sin of missing the mark of God's perfection caused an inseparable divide between them and their loving Father. The now unholy was removed from the Most Holy God.[8]

Yet, God had a plan…

God would come to rescue humanity and He would take upon Himself the penalty for the curse of their sin and the devil's evil. Jesus came as a man to call back to the Father those who had turned from Him.

Jesus, co-equal, co-divine, co-eternal, and co-existent with the Father and the Holy Spirit, gave up the prerogatives of His Kingdom to live among man and reveal the love of God.[9] He healed the sick, raised the dead, set captives free from the enemy's tyranny, and literally brought heaven down to earth.

In accordance with the God-given Old Testament animal sacrifices—the shedding of life-giving blood to atone for man's sin—Jesus shed His own sinless blood on the cross. His once-for-all sacrifice paid the penalty for the sin of humankind.[10] And by His resurrection from the dead, Jesus defeated death, making eternal life available to anyone who receives Him into their lives *by faith*.[11] This act of faith by a person, also paves the way for a new life, new beginnings from their past, and heart and mind transformation.[12]

All of this done by His Holy Spirit taking up residence in the human soul and breathing life into their once dead spirit. Indeed, spiritual CPR![13]

To receive Jesus into your life is a life-altering decision. You will no longer walk alone.[14] You will have the resources of heaven on your side.[15] You can walk intimately with the God of the universe and no longer search for life's meaning or purpose–you will find His purposes for you are thrilling and fulfilling. You will discover that His presence is more than enough to satisfy every longing, and His power is available to strengthen you from the inside-out and will provide all that you need.[16] Though you and I still live in a broken, fallen, and disease-riddled world, the power of the enemy over our lives can be decimated at the name of Jesus.[17] The Lord Jesus still heals and works wonders today.[18]

Still, the choice is given to every man, woman, or child to receive the Savior's free gift of eternal life by faith. He will not force Himself upon you.

If you have not done so before, please don't hesitate to take this most important step of inviting Jesus into your life. By asking Him to be Lord of all you are–even if your faith seems small–is the best decision you will ever make in your lifetime.

> *He who finds his life will lose it, and he who loses his life*
> *for My sake will find it.*

Matthew 10:39

If you are ready to receive the Lord Jesus into your life, but you are not sure what to say to Him, simply pray the words below, making them your own in your heart and mind.

> *Dear Lord Jesus,*
>
> *I come to you now in great need. I ask to be born again in Your Holy Spirit. Please forgive all my sin. I acknowledge that You died on the cross to save me and You rose again that I might live with you now and*

*forever. I receive You into my heart, and I offer my life
to You.*

In Your Powerful Name, I pray, Lord Jesus.

Amen.

Please let me know if you prayed this prayer! I would love to send you an easy to read Bible and a simple to do Bible Study to introduce you to the marvelous adventure in Jesus that you have just embarked upon. You can contact me through my website at **www.sueboldt.com** or by email at **sue@sueboldt.com**.

*But as many as received Him, to them He gave the right
to become children of God, to those who believe in His
name.*

John 1:12

5

Power in His Word

For the word of God is living and powerful,
and sharper than any two-edged sword,
piercing even to the division of soul and spirit,
and of joints and marrow,
and is a discerner of the thoughts and intents of the heart.

Hebrews 4:12

Make no mistake about it, God is always speaking.[1] However, just like someone who is trying to contact you by phone, until you do your little part and pick up the call or read their text, you may never know what they wanted to share with you.

God's Word, the Bible, is the Lord's main avenue of communication to us. Yes, He can use anything to speak to us, but the Bible is the litmus test for what His voice sounds like and what He has to say.[2] And we won't know any of those amazing words He has to tell us if we don't answer His *phone call* and read His book for ourselves.

The Bible is a book like no other. The words on its pages are the very life-breath of God, breathing wholeness, salvation, deliverance, and healing for the whole person–body, soul, and spirit.[3]

We open God's Word to learn about our magnificent Creator–His ways, His character, and His purposes. We read it to learn how best to navigate through life in this darkened world and take authority over its evil ruler and his demonic minions.[4] The Bible and its advice on how to live were never meant to kill fun or happiness. Instead, they are an invitation to a way of life filled with beyond reason peace, hope, joy, salvation, and healing.

This Living Book's words will spare us from much that the prince of darkness wants to throw at us. Like the covering of an umbrella, when we position ourselves under the Word's guidelines, we will miss much of the junk and evil the world and its ruler want to dish out.[5] We may get *splashed* at times because we live in this hell-bent world, but living life the way God prescribes protects us from so much. Following His commands–basically to love others and love Him with all our hearts[6]–keeps us in alignment with Him to receive all that He has promised us as His children.

The Bible contains God's truth to overcome every lie we believe about ourselves and God, every untruth the world would throw at us, and the devil's deception.[7]

When we approach God's Word as a living and breathing book that speaks to us today, it provides the spiritual oxygen to guide, correct, comfort, and teach us. We learn from its pages how to walk in Holy Spirit power and build our faith. It is *not only* our oxygen; it is our *daily bread*. Reading it feeds our spirit, encourages, strengthens, heals us, and provides us with our God-given authority over any challenging situation we may face as we declare its truth in Jesus' name.

We come to this book to learn more about the Lord and to hear His voice speaking directly into our current circumstances. When we come to partake of its riches, we are drawn into the presence of Jesus, the Living Word.[8]

> *And the **Word** became flesh and dwelt among us,and we behold His glory, the glory as of the only begotten of the Father, full of grace and truth.*

> John 1:14 (emphasis, mine)

The original Greek New Testament word in this passage describing Jesus as the Word of God, is *logos*. Its meaning includes *the transmission of something being said, a thought, a communication, a discourse, or a speech.* Logos is the word used for *divine declarations, precepts, instruction, doctrine, and promises.*

The Lord Jesus is the *Living Logos.* As we make a daily habit of coming to the feast of God's Word and inviting the Holy Spirit to reveal Jesus to us, we are steadily transformed.[9]

A Rhema Word...

There is also another Greek word used in the New Testament for *word.*

> *And take the helmet of salvation, and the sword of the Spirit, which is the **word** of God;*
>
> Ephesians 6:17 (emphasis, mine)

A *rhema* word is one of the pieces of God's Armor found in *Ephesians 6:10-18.* This type of word, differing from logos, is our offensive weapon—our sword in the Spirit—used to encourage us and defeat the devil and any circumstance that would overwhelm us, including an illness. I consider the *Isaiah 41* passage that spoke to my heart in the mountains and has stayed with me through my healing journey as a rhema word.

The English translation of this Hebrew word, *rhema,* is *to speak, a statement, or a word uttered by a living voice.*

The *New Spirit-Filled Life Bible* states it this way...

> *In reference to the Bible, **logos** is the Bible in its entirety; **rhema** is a verse from the Bible. The meaning of rhema in distinction to logos is illustrated in Ephesians 6:17, where the reference is not to the Scriptures as a whole, but to that portion which the believer wields as a sword in time of need.*[10]

A rhema word from God is a *now* word, for a current or coming situation. It is a divine encouragement or weapon from God in our moment of need. Jesus, when facing the great temptation in the wilderness, spoke a rhema word to the tempter directly from the Scriptures:

*But He answered and said, "It is written, 'Man shall not
live by bread alone, but by every **word** that proceeds
from the mouth of God.'"*

Matthew 4:4 (emphasis, mine)

We can learn from the Lord's example of using the authority of God's Word
as the weapon of our warfare. In fact, the Greek word used in the
passage above *is rhema*, not logos. Jesus shows us how to employ a Spirit-
directed Bible passage to declare God's dominion, truth, and power when
we face an illness or any difficult situation. Knowing God's Word for
ourselves and reading it expectantly to hear His voice for our lives can
change everything for us.

It is a very subjective matter in discerning when God is giving you a direct
Scripture–a rhema word–for your given situation, including a health issue.
Indeed, anyone can pull out a verse from the Bible and make it say what they
want. There is a danger in doing that, and certainly, that has led to an abuse
of God's Word for misguided purposes. Nevertheless, the rewards of
someone sensing in their spirit that God is giving them a specific word for
their situation is greater than the few people who would attempt to twist His
Word to their own desires.

Both Paul and James give us a clear idea of what the Lord's voice sounds
like, with James making a clear distinction between the enemy's and the
world's voices, and God's voice:

*Finally, brethren, whatever things are true, whatever
things are noble, whatever things are just, whatever
things are pure, whatever things are lovely, whatever
things are of good report, if there is any virtue and if
there is anything praiseworthy--meditate on these things.*

Philippians 4:8

*This wisdom does not descend from above, but is earthly,
sensual, demonic.*

> *For where envy and self-seeking exist, confusion and every evil thing are there.*
>
> ***But the wisdom that is from above*** *is first pure, then peaceable, gentle, willing to yield, full of mercy and good fruits, without partiality and without hypocrisy.*

James 3:15-17 (emphasis, mine)

Everything about our walk with the Lord Jesus is about faith. It may require baby steps of faith on our part to recognize if He truly is giving us a portion of scripture to strengthen us and to use in spiritual warfare prayer.

Ask yourself these questions to help determine if the Lord is giving you a rhema word for your situation:

- Does the passage strike a chord in my emotions? Your heart might be warmed by it, or you sense hope or joy. Even difficult-to-hear words from the Lord are infused with His love.

- Do I feel confusion and a lack of peace, or does this verse encourage and strengthen me?

- Am I receiving greater clarity about my situation that is giving me peace?

- How does the passage line up with what Paul and James wrote about hearing God's voice?

- Is this passage so out of alignment with the rest of God's Word that I am manipulating it?

- What do my spiritual mentors and pastors sense about this portion of God's Word in regard to my situation?

Knowing whether the Lord is giving you a rhema word takes practice and faith, meaning that you may just have to start somewhere.

The next time a portion of God's word touches your heart, answer the questions above, then apply what is speaking to you and trust it. The Bible even states we must *exercise* stepping out in faith in His Word to grow in greater discernment about what is from God and what isn't.[11]

This Marvelous Book is filled with many healing stories and verses to encourage your faith and provide the ammunition needed to bind any spirit of infirmity or physical malady as you seek the Lord for His healing touch. In the final chapter of this book, you will find several verses written out about strength, hope, and healing to encourage you. Open His Word and your heart to see if any of these passages resonate with you, or even better, open the Bible for yourself to find the comfort, joy, or healing you need.

The *phone* is ringing, and Jesus is calling you. Take the time to answer His call and hear what He desires to share with you.

6

Holy Spirit Overflow

I indeed baptize you with water unto repentance,
but He who is coming after me is mightier than I,
whose sandals I am not worthy to carry.
He will baptize you with the Holy Spirit and fire.

Matthew 3:11

All four Gospel accounts in the New Testament–*Matthew, Mark, Luke, and John*–record John the Baptist's words in the verse above. Although Christian believers have differing opinions on whether the second experience of Holy Spirit baptism ended with the first-century church, the fact remains that Christians need this experience more than ever before in these troubled days we live in.

When seeking God's direction for healing through a difficult diagnosis, the aid of the third Person of the Trinity, the Holy Spirit, is beneficial beyond words.

A careful examination of the Scriptures and church history reveals that Lord Jesus intends for every one of His followers to not only experience the indwelling of the Holy Spirit at salvation, but also the second experience of Spirit empowerment found in Acts.[1] The disciples received the Holy Spirit immediately after the resurrection, yet Jesus instructed them to wait for a second enduement of His power.[2]

Jesus is the same yesterday, today, and forever[3] and His ministry and working in the lives of humankind has never ceased. He still saves today, heals today, delivers today, and His Holy Spirit still indwells His children today.

Peter declared in his first sermon following the outpouring of the Holy Spirit on the day of Pentecost:

> *...and you shall receive the gift of the Holy Spirit.*
>
> *For the promise is to you and to your children, and to all who are afar off, as many as the Lord our God will call.*

Acts 2:38-39

Peter begins his sermon with reference to the prophet Joel's account of the Holy Spirit's outpouring upon all people during the end times. Peter compared that passage to what had just taken place for the 120 in the upper room, also quoting Jesus' words about receiving the promise of the Holy Spirit in *Luke 24:49*.[4] His words tell us that *all people* who would respond to the gospel through the ages could experience what had just taken place for the believers in Jerusalem.

The original Greek word for baptism is *baptizo*, which means *to baptize, dip, dye, immerse, plunge, submerge, inundate, flood, swamp, soak, douse, drench, and saturate*. Ponder each of these words for a moment.

We recognize the definition of *baptizo* in the sense of water baptism, but apply it now to an experience with the Holy Spirit's baptism–the same Holy Spirit who already lives within every believer. Such a wonder![5] And with this wonder of Holy Spirit baptism comes a release of spiritual power and ability, enabling a Christian to do and know things beyond their natural abilities just as we read in the *Book of Acts*.[6]

One of these marvelous gifts is a spiritual prayer language, often called in the scriptures, the *gift of speaking in tongues*. This gift of an unknown language is given to the believer directly from the Holy Spirit living inside them. It strengthens the speaker and provides them with a vocabulary beyond themselves in prayer and worship.[7] This language is a huge benefit at any time in a Christian's life, but it is especially helpful while confronting sickness.

The Spirit's Release

The Scriptures clearly tell us that every person who has received Jesus as Lord is one of His children. They have experienced being born again of the Spirit; their once dead spirit is now filled with the Holy Spirit.[8] With this truth established, how does one receive the baptism or overflow of the Spirit and the subsequent gifts He offers? In this chapter, I am referring to the gift of speaking in tongues. The answer is to simply ask our loving Father.

> *If a son asks for bread from any father among you, will he give him a stone? Or if he asks for a fish, will he give him a serpent instead of a fish?*
>
> *Or if he asks for an egg, will he offer him a scorpion?*
>
> *If you then, being evil, know how to give good gifts to your children, how much more will your heavenly Father give the Holy Spirit to those who ask Him!*
>
> Luke 11:11-13

After praying for hundreds of individuals to receive the baptism in the Holy Spirit, I have come to realize that many people have already experienced Him in this manner. However, they often didn't know what had taken place, or they were not aware of His gifts, including a new spiritual prayer language. Frequently, this overflow of the Spirit took place when the person came to a point of surrender to the Lord. They may have sensed a physical warmth in their being, a feeling of peace, or an awareness of God's nearness, but they just didn't know what was happening.

I know this is true because of my own experience with Spirit baptism. I had a powerful physical sense of His overflow, but I did not speak in a spiritual language until six months later. A more mature Christian than myself had to explain to me from the Scriptures what had taken place.

On the other hand, many who have asked for prayer to receive the Spirit's overflow have doubted their experience because they either didn't have any physical sensation, or they didn't receive their spiritual gift of prayer language at that time. Nonetheless, they most likely received His empowerment.

We must take Jesus' words in *Luke 11:11-13* at face value. Just as we receive Him into our lives by faith, we also welcome the Holy Spirit's second experience by faith.

A person at the point of their salvation may have had a physical or emotional response, or maybe they felt nothing at all, and the same is true for receiving the Spirit baptism. We receive His work and gifts in our lives *by faith*, whether we have an experience or not. If we don't initially have a physical response, it will come later, as we learn to cultivate and nurture God's presence in our times alone with Him.

Asking Him to Come...

If you are uncertain whether you have received this second marvelous gift of the Holy Spirit, now is the time to take a small step of faith and ask Him for it. It is really that simple.

I was once taught that a Christian had to have all his ducks in a row and have their lives squeaky clean before receiving the Holy Spirit's baptism, however that is not the truth of the Bible. We come because *we cannot* get our lives squeaky clean on our own, and we need all the power and aid He can give us. This is especially true when we are physically or emotionally weak. We simply come to our Father as we did at salvation and we ask to experience this blessing just as Jesus told us to do.

I encourage you to first read through the remainder of this chapter, then go back over it when you are ready to have your prayer time.

Find a quiet place where you will not be interrupted for several minutes. Draw your heart close to the Lord Jesus in worship and adoration. It is helpful to speak words of adoration quietly out loud to better aid your concentration. Beginning to talk out loud will also help you later if you are seeking to receive your prayer language because you will already be in a place of speaking.

With the help of the Holy Spirit (He wants this more for you than you do!), focus your thoughts upon the Lord's loveliness and beauty. Reread the previous passage from *Luke 11:11-13* to encourage your faith.

When you are ready, expectantly ask your Heavenly Father for the baptism in the Holy Spirit.

As you continue to whisper your praise and receive the overflow of the Spirit, enjoy the quiet of the moment. Sit in the stillness of His presence with your mind and heart fixed upon Him. Don't hurry or rush this time. On the basis of your request and your faith—even if it is mustard seed small—you have received the baptism in the Holy Spirit.

Now, continue to thank Him *with your voice* for the wonderful Gift He has given you!

> *For all the promises of God in Him are Yes, and in Him*
> *Amen, to the glory of God through us.*
>
> 2 Corinthians 1:20

If you are ready to receive the Holy Spirit's language—with no guilt or shame if you are not ready—once again, you simply ask for this gift. Quite literally say out loud in your own words something like, *Lord, I desire to speak in tongues now.* Next, start speaking out loud. Just as you were already speaking words of praise, now the Holy Spirit will give you a new vocabulary *as you speak out loud your new language.* Your voice doesn't have to be loud, just loud enough for you to hear yourself.

It is imperative that you *speak out loud.* I cannot stress this enough. The Spirit within you wants to pray, and you are giving Him your voice.

What you are doing is similar to Peter's experience of faith when he desired to walk on water just as Jesus was doing.[9] The Lord, in response to Peter, asked Peter to step out of the boat and walk on water with Him. Jesus didn't yank Peter out of the vessel. *Peter had to take the first step and swing his leg over the side of the boat.* In the same manner, the Holy Spirit won't grab your tongue and make you talk. I have rarely, if ever, seen or heard of that taking place. Instead, you are cooperating with the Holy Spirit by taking the first step as you begin to speak out syllables or phrases that you do not know or understand. The Holy Spirit *will* take over! Yes, really!

If you start to speak but seem to freeze up, then speak any type of syllable that is not English or a known language to you. *You are swinging your leg over the boat, just like Peter.* It can be a simple consonant and vowel combination, just speak it out and keep going. Your words may seem slow and halting, or you may have fast-paced staccato-sounding words. You may have thoughts of unknown syllables–speak out what you are thinking. Regardless, the Holy Spirit has answered your prayer, and He is praying through you! Don't let your intellect or understanding rob you of this great gift. The learned and intellectual apostle Paul didn't.[10]

This is the point of Spirit baptism prayer where a person may think they didn't receive either the baptism in the Holy Spirit or their prayer language. However, this is not the case. By faith, you have received them. If someone waits for the Spirit to move their tongue, nothing will happen.

We see that on the day of Pentecost, the early disciples *began to speak*, and then the Spirit gave them the words. The same is true for us.

> *And they were all filled with the Holy Spirit and began to speak with other tongues, as the Spirit gave them utterance.*

> Acts 2:4

This is an excellent point of surrender. You are trusting the Lord that He has baptized you in the Holy Spirit according to His Word. You are surrendering your voice to the Lord. You are also offering your thoughts to Him by not trying to analyze your new language.

If you stop to try and get a handle on what you are doing in these early stages of your new vocabulary, you might not continue. Paul told us that our prayer language is beyond our understanding, so don't even try to figure it out![11] This is a spiritual gift, not a natural one. Keep going.

The new language you are enjoying is the Holy Spirit speaking directly to heaven's throne room, worshiping and praising God, and praying prayers that you won't often understand. Don't be concerned if you only have a few words, or you seem to be repeating the same words; it is still the Holy Spirit praying through you. The more you keep your mind and heart fixed on Jesus, and not over-thinking what is happening, the easier it will be. You will relax as time progresses, and your spiritual vocabulary will grow by the Holy Spirit's doing, not yours.

If you struggle with your prayer language, I encourage you to continue. Those who have experienced this struggle have had to get past the hurdle of their own thinking by pressing onward. Then, their spiritual language became smooth sailing as they continued often, with their confidence growing that the Holy Spirit was genuinely speaking and not themselves.

You can stop and start your prayer language at any time, and it will never leave you. Having this gift from the Lord will strengthen you on your healing journey. When I was in excruciating pain in the emergency room, I relied upon my spiritual language and I rely upon it every single day of my life now. What comfort and strength! Having your spiritual language is a huge benefit and aid to silencing the enemy, positioning you to hear the Lord's voice for your situation, and the ability to pray when you are not sure what to ask. Paul tells us…

> *For he who speaks in a tongue does not speak to men but to God, for no one understands him; however, in the spirit he speaks mysteries...He who speaks in a tongue edifies himself…*

1 Corinthians 14:2,4

Daily Overflow...

As you move on from this moment, how do you maintain this fullness of the Spirit? Make time regularly to sit in the Lord's presence as you are now. We will discuss this in the next chapter. Pray in your prayer language often throughout the day, every day.

> *On the last day, that great day of the feast, Jesus stood and cried out, saying, "If anyone thirsts, let him come to Me and drink.*
>
> *He who believes in Me, as the Scripture has said, out of his heart will flow rivers of living water."*
>
> *But this He spoke concerning the Spirit, whom those believing in Him would receive; for the Holy Spirit was not yet given, because Jesus was not yet glorified.*

John 7:37-39

Please do not make the mistake that I did for years of thinking that this beautiful overflow of God's Spirit is a one-time event. The Holy Spirit desires for us to encounter Him again and again every day of our lives as Paul wrote about in *Ephesians 5:18.*[12]

First and foremost, Holy Spirit baptism was promised by God to Jesus' followers for strength, courage, wisdom, supernatural ability, and giftings to preach the Gospel to the world. You will discover greater discernment and sensitivity to what the Lord desires to work through you to reach others. And yet, the Spirit's power and gifts are for your benefit too, a powerful tool in drawing closer to The Great Healer, the Lord Jesus Christ.

7

Cultivating God's Presence

You will show me the path of life;
In Your presence is fullness of joy;
At Your right hand are pleasures forevermore.

Psalm 16:11

When the sun was setting,
all those who had any that were sick with
various diseases brought them to Him;
and He laid His hands on every one of them
and healed them.

Luke 4:40

Let's get one thing on the table. None of us are deserving of anything, including healing from the good hand of God. We all have stuff, and we know our faults and failings firsthand. Right? Yet Jesus invites us to come and sit with Him. We come, *not* because we have all life's answers figured out, *but because we don't.* We come, *not* because our faith in God is perfect; we *come because it is often woefully lacking.* The Bible tells us over and over again that He wants us to come to Him and be filled with His presence in the Holy Spirit.[1]

> *Behold, I stand at the door and knock. If anyone hears*
> *My voice and opens the door, I will come in to him and*
> *dine with him, and he with Me.*

Revelation 3:20

Not long ago, an older woman in our church was struggling with Parkinson's disease. She had uncontrollable tremors in her hands, and she was beginning to lose the ability to walk. Connie was in her eighties when her daughter, Eileen, led Connie to Christ as her Savior.

One day, Connie, in her simple, start-up faith, asked Jesus to heal her from Parkinson's disease, just like He had healed me of stage 4 cancer. She had been sitting in her room alone with the Lord in a quiet time. Connie told Eileen that she saw Jesus enter her room, walk over to her, and heal her. She came to the church service the following Sunday and held out her hands for everyone to see the tremors that had once hindered her were gone entirely. Then, Connie walked to the front of the church sanctuary. Previously, she could only lean onto others to shuffle along—a real miracle. Connie was the talk of her senior exercise class the following week!

About eighteen months later, Connie was diagnosed with liver cancer. This time around, Connie had peace that it was time for her to go be with the Lord, and she was looking forward to her grand homecoming! How could she fear when the One who had proved His love to her in so many ways was leading the way? Her son-in-law would check on Connie each evening when he arrived home from work. *How are you doing?* He asked. Connie would raise one of her hands and wave, always responding with a smile on her face, *Just waiting!* With loved ones surrounding her, she soon was in the embrace of her Beloved.

Even though Connie was a brand-new believer, she spent time alone with her Savior, getting to know Him.

There is nothing like taking the time to get to know someone well. There is no substitute for spending time with a person, conversing back and forth, and getting to understand who they are and what they are like. When life is experienced together in a deep relationship, it is so much more meaningful and fulfilling than what only a casual acquaintance can bring. When we take the time to invest in a relationship, and we feel comfortable with the person, trust is built. The same is true with Lord Jesus.

We can attend church, read our Bibles, pray, and still only have a cursory relationship with the Lord. We can live a Christian life that is more theory than experience, and when trial or tragedy comes, we can easily get walloped and sidelined by anxiety or worry. When bad news takes place in any area of our lives, or a difficult diagnosis happens, we can forget how much Jesus loves us and that He has positioned us in Him. We may find ourselves unprepared to take action against our enemy in prayer.

This was me. I loved the Lord at an early age and experienced the overflow of the Holy Spirit in my young teens. Not long after, I had a profound encounter with Him that confirmed His reality and heaven's certainty. Nevertheless, as a young wife, mom, and church planter with my husband, the busyness of life, kids, work, and church drowned out the close intimacy I had experienced with the Lord in my youth. During this time, my struggles with an eating disorder and an uncontrollable thought-life led me into a mild depression.

My Christian to-do lists became more important to me than taking the time to get real and raw with Jesus, pour out my heart, and then wait for what He had to say. I read God's Word daily, but often in preparation to teach others or not feel guilty. I usually didn't experience His living presence while reading His Word, or when I did, I sabotaged what He was saying to me by listening and believing what others or the world was speaking.

Still, God, in His infinite faithfulness, delivered me from my depression and eating disorder and I received physical healing for a chronic gastric issue. Nevertheless, I lived a Christian life of mountain-top experiences at events or retreats, only to head down to the valley of daily living in-between times. I loved the *highs* of Christian living, but I couldn't seem to maintain them. I spent more time in the wilderness or dry bones of life instead of walking in the Holy Spirit's presence and power.

Only a few years before my bout with cancer, I realized I'd had enough of living a less-than Christian life. My quiet times changed. I threw out my laundry list of prayer requests, and I began to linger in this precious time until I had a physical sense of His presence. By this, I mean a sense of calm or peace, or bubbling joy, power, or well-being, that only God's presence can give.[2]

It also meant not leaving this time alone with Him until I received a fresh *rhema* word from His Word or sensed the soft impression of His voice upon my heart that always coincided with what the Bible teaches. I not only read about His love for me; I began to *feel and know* it for myself, increasing my faith. From the place of His peace, I seemed to be more in tune with how the Holy Spirit would direct me in prayer and battle in Jesus' name. The rewards in every area and level of my life were immediate just as He said.

> *But you, when you pray, go into your room, and when you have shut your door, pray to your Father who is in the **secret place**; and your Father who sees in secret will reward you openly.*
>
> Matthew 6:6 (emphasis, mine)

My desire to be still and know God had ramifications for myself, and others as well.[3] The life-long stronghold in my thought-life broke. Ordered thinking was restored to me, bringing freedom I had sought for years. And, within six months of starting this practice, my father, our oldest daughter, and my atheist coworker had encounters with Jesus and surrendered their lives to Him.

How does this apply to healing?

There is something a person can't help but notice when they read about Jesus' life in the New Testament. In His presence, *people were healed.* He brought physical, spiritual, emotional, mental healing, and wholeness. He cast out demonic oppression and spirits of infirmity that also inflicted physical maladies.[4] The same is true today...

> *Jesus Christ is the same yesterday, today, and forever.*
>
> Hebrews 13:8

We take our cue from the Lord Himself. Jesus often spent time alone with His Father and His earthly ministry appears to flow from these times of sweet communion.[5] Jesus used varying methods to minster healing, with no set formula except the leading of the Holy Spirit and what the Father was speaking.[6]

During these *secret place* times with the Lord, my faith grew because I was encountering Him. Please understand, I came—and still come to Him—warts and all. I come because I am so needy and not perfect.

Don't let the enemy lie to you that you are unworthy to be with Jesus. Yes, we are unworthy on our own merit, but we now belong to Him, and He has clothed us in His righteousness and opened wide the door for us to share life with Him. He has completely forgiven our sins, even when our inadequacies are glaring at us.[7]

It was during one of these sweet times at our family cabin that the Lord gave me a head's up of what was to come, and He filled my heart and mind with His promises. Later, when a few moments of anxiety tried to creep in, getting alone with the Savior and not leaving until I had His peace beyond understanding, spared me much anguish when cancer returned two more times.

When we cultivate Jesus' felt presence in our lives through the Holy Spirit who indwells us, we make room for His healing touch. In these times of seeking Him, we sense His nearness, His love, and His power. When we hear His voice through His Word, our faith increases[8]

A benefit of these times alone with Him is the renewing of our minds.[9] We learn to silence the thoughts of guilt, accusation, doubt, and worry because we are learning—slowly at first—to control our thoughts. When the Lord gives us a directive, whether to follow a physician's treatment plan, take a natural approach, or forgo medicine altogether, we can act upon it with confidence. For instance, when I felt led by the Lord to stop the chemotherapy medication at one point, and then again when seeking a third surgery later on in my journey.

As we learn to hear His voice in our lives, there may be times that Jesus tells us we need to ask forgiveness of someone, or we may need to forgive a wrong. He may let us know that our critical thoughts and words are hindering our healing. Maybe He reveals to us we have sin in our lives that we have shoved under the carpet that has allowed our adversary to gain access to our health. The Holy Spirit may direct us to take action, and as we are obedient, the healing will come.[10] We may receive a directive to fast[11] for a period of time and come against the work of a spirit of infirmity in our body.[12] Or, when healing seems delayed, the Lord may tell us to rest and trust.

It is imperative that we take the baby steps of *time with Jesus* we need to learn His voice for ourselves and take the baby steps of *faith* to do what He says.

Be encouraged to get your eyes off your healing and simply onto the Lord. I know that seems almost impossible to do when severe physical pain is in play or the medications you are taking are distracting. But all Jesus asks is that we come. He can take care of the things that may trouble or distract us. It is never too late to draw close to Him.[13]

Yes, we need to spend time and touch base daily with the Lord when we bring Him our prayer requests and open His Word to study it and to speak to us. Paul, the apostle, also encourages us to talk to Him all through our day, every day.[14] What is being shared in this chapter is a separate time where we come, just like Joshua, King David, or Mary, Martha's sister, in the New Testament.[15] Like them, we come to behold the beauty of God and cultivate the sense of His presence through the Holy Spirit who lives in us. Our spiritual language will be a benefit during these times.

> *One thing I have desired of the LORD,*
> *That will I seek:*
> *That I may dwell in the house of the LORD*
> *All the days of my life,*
> *To behold the beauty of the LORD,*
> *And to inquire in His temple.*

Psalm 27:4

O God, You are my God;
Early will I seek You…

So I have looked for You in the sanctuary,
To see Your power and Your glory.

Psalm 63:1-2

Did you notice the second passage was written while David was in the wilderness? How fitting that David had already made a life-practice of being in God's presence so that when trials came, he already knew where to meet God and experience His power and glory.

Practical Tips for 'Secret Place' Times…

Just as you would protect a young seedling from the elements that would destroy it, we need to learn how to cultivate and nurture a quiet time alone with Jesus without distraction.

I didn't always succeed, and I still don't at times! Nevertheless, I just keep coming back to this time of lingering with Him, at least once a week, or whenever I sense His peace or joy waning inside of me. I have learned that it isn't selfish to say, *Please, fill me up, Lord!* Instead, I perceive His sheer delight when I come to Him as my Abba-Daddy and as a joint-heir with Christ.[16]

When taking time to be with Jesus, even when I'm maintaining a crazy schedule or traveling, circumstances no longer have the power to rock my world. I no longer need to work at *doing* ministry; people want what I have. Because of nurturing the Lord's presence in stillness and expectancy before Him, I haven't suffered the burn-out that once was regularly a part of my life. Here are some other practical steps:

- **Put on your calendar scheduled times alone with God like you would your best friend**. Give yourself a good half-hour or more. Without adding to your plate of to-dos, this is not your everyday time with Jesus; this is a separate time to worship and wait upon Him and hear what He has to say. Not the other way around.

- **The best time to meet with Jesus is when you are at your best.** Pastor Wayne Cordeiro shares this encouragement in his book, *Divine Mentor*.[17] When are you most awake? Morning, afternoon, or evening? Make that your time to schedule being with the Lord.

- **Arrange for someone to watch the kids, dogs, duties, or whatever requires your oversight, so that you will have uninterrupted time.**

- **Put your phone in another room and remove every distraction possible.** Bring a notebook if it helps to jot down some stray, but important reminders that come to your thoughts, so you don't start obsessing about what you might forget. Crazy, but true. Don't be discouraged if training your thoughts to stay on Jesus takes practice! We all get distracted, but His Holy Spirit will help us. We just need to come.

- **Get comfortable.** Bring your Bible and a journal to record what you think He is saying to you from His Word and His heart.[18] You will often want to go back and remind yourself of what He has spoken to you.

- **Keep it simple.** Ask Jesus to join you. Truthfully, He has been waiting for you! There is no magic formula, and if there were, your time alone with the Lord would become just another to-do list from religiosity. Instead, you are waiting for the Holy Spirit's leading.

- **Worship.** Worship focuses our heart and mind on the Lord and attunes us to His presence.[19] Pastor Randy Remington states: *worship interrupts our preoccupation with ourselves.*[20] The psalms are great for worship inspiration. Try softly–or loudly!– singing your favorite praise and worship songs or worship in your spiritual language. For some, playing worship music is helpful, but don't let it become distracting if you use your phone.

- **Let the Holy Spirit lead you.** We not only cultivate experiencing the Lord's presence, we are also growing in letting the Spirit lead us, too. We are learning to be continually filled to overflowing with Him in our lives. Take baby steps. If a thought comes to mind–a picture or a Bible verse–what do you think the Lord is saying to you? [21] One thing might lead to something else, or one Bible verse might reference another until you land where Jesus is leading you. You will seldom lack knowing God's will for your life when you make these quiet times your priority.[22]

- **Don't get discouraged your first time.** Like priming the pump on a deep well that we haven't drawn water from for a long time, it may take a few meetups before the dust is knocked off our spirit. Remember, the Lord desires this time with you more than you do!

No one can do this for you. Spending quality time with the Savior enables us to grow in sensitivity to the Holy Spirit to hear how to proceed when we are in physical distress. Remaining in His continual presence causes the catastrophes of life to seem much smaller *because they are*. We can stay ready in His company, and should a trial come of any nature, fear already has no place in our lives. When we hear from the Lord for ourselves, no one can take His words, promises, peace, joy, or direction away from us.[23]

We can be healed in His Presence.

Chapter 7

8

When Healing is Delayed

*Now may the God of hope
fill you with all joy and peace in believing,
that you may abound in hope by the power of the Holy Spirit.*

Romans 15:13

There is healing in the presence of the Lord and in His incomprehensible sacrifice on the cross. *By His stripes we are healed.* But sometimes, the manifestation of healing may be on hold. Let's take a *brief* look at a few possible hindrances to healing. A list of resources for your further study is provided at the back of this book.

A Few Hindrances…

We see in the New Testament various times where Jesus could not heal folks due to their **unbelief**. Knowing this stops many of us, including myself, in our tracks. Who has enough faith? This side of heaven, I am not sure if anyone truly has perfect faith. It can be a source of guilt, blame, and shame, especially in regard to physical healing.

There are at least three types of faith:

- A tiny bit of faith that is shaky at best.

- A growing faith that we build as we trust Jesus more and more for the situations in our lives.

- A Holy Spirit gift of faith. A supernatural endowment beyond our *growing* faith.

Regarding healing, genuine faith is more than trying to will something to happen or having *faith in our faith*. It is more than praying for healing or an answered prayer. The bedrock of our faith must stand upon a solid assurance that *God is good and He loves me*. When we *rest* in real-deal faith, fear has little to no grip upon us, no matter what happens.

> *There is no fear in love; but perfect love casts out fear,*
> *because fear involves torment. But he who fears has not*
> *been made perfect in love.*

1 John 4:18

When we face any trial in life, including physical illness, our faith can be tested, and I think most of us realize that we come up short in the faith department. We almost all believe that God can heal, but the question is, *will He?* Instead of trying to stir something up in ourselves, these are the times we must come to our Savior and humbly ask, as in the Bible with the apostles and the father whose child was sick, *Lord, I believe, help my unbelief!*[1] Honesty with the Lord for where we are truly at with our faith, or lack of it, is always the best route and gives the Holy Spirit something to work with.

Our faith *can* be built, one step at a time. Be encouraged to remember from previous chapters, that our faith…

- grows as we read, meditate upon, and apply God's Word to our lives.

- is edified or built up when we pray in our spiritual language.

- becomes stronger as we become certain of God's reality by cultivating His presence in our alone times with Him.

We see from the Scriptures that there are other aspects of our lives that can interfere with God's healing work. It may be time to ask the Holy Spirit to help us do a little housecleaning and examine our hearts.[2] We must see if we are harboring *unforgiveness or unconfessed sin*.[3] This isn't said to place blame or guilt but we have to be truthful about where we are at emotionally, mentally, and spiritually.

Not being able to forgive someone, including not being able to let go of a past wound, hurt, or trauma, can open the door to physical issues in our body. No, this isn't always the case but certainly science testifies to this Biblical truth.[4] Experiences from our past may put undue stress, worry, strife, and discord in our bodies.

The Lord not only purchased our physical healing, the power of the cross and resurrection secures our emotional, mental, and of course spiritual healing, as well.[5] When we come to an area of life where forgiveness or healing from a past incident is needed, we can come confidently to the Great Physician in our time of need.[6] This is too important to neglect or brush aside. What is taking place in our souls—our heart, mind, and personality—can be the cause of our illness now, or it can be exacerbating it.

> *For we do not have a High Priest who cannot sympathize with our weaknesses, but was in all points tempted as we are, yet without sin.*
>
> *Let us therefore come boldly to the throne of grace, that we may obtain mercy and find grace to help in time of need.*
>
> Hebrews 4:15-16

Unforgiveness and healing for our past may seem overwhelming to tackle, but as with anything in Jesus, we rely completely on Him for His guidance and direction. Seek any necessary help and prayer that you need with a wise, trusted Christian friend, your pastor, or a Christian counselor. Know that freedom in Christ is possible. *(A list of resources is supplied at the end of this book.)*

Finally, have we allowed sin in our lives that may have cracked open the door to allow our flesh or our adversary to mess with our health?

Remember, we live in a fallen, broken, and evil world ruled by a cruel prince until Jesus returns. We still get hit with hard things and calamities, but with the enormous difference that we have authority in Jesus' name to overturn situations. And we have the great gift of a relationship with the Lord Jesus who will hold our hand and either walk us through life's trials, walk over them, or He will completely deliver us from them.

These things I have spoken to you, that in Me you may have peace. In the world you will have tribulation; but be of good cheer, I have overcome the world.

John 16:33

Nevertheless, when we continue in the stuff of life that is opposite of God's pure love, design, and communion with Him, we *can* step out from under the covering of His authority and power in our lives. God isn't giving us a list of rules to quench our fun, instead He is lovingly sharing with us how to navigate and reign in life with the least amount of harm brought on by our foolishness.[7]

He said, "If you will listen carefully to the voice of the LORD your God and do what is right in his sight, obeying his commands and keeping all his decrees, then I will not make you suffer any of the diseases I sent on the Egyptians; for I am the LORD who heals you."

Exodus 15:26

So, it might be time to take care of some business with God. If areas of your life have come to your mind where you know you have been stepping out of His covering and best for you, take time now to make things right:

- Confess your sin, He is faithful and just to completely forgive you.[8]

- Remember, Jesus has covered all your messes, past, present, and future. You can't ever earn or work for His love, simply receive it.[9]

- Don't allow guilt or condemnation to overtake you, because that's not from God.[10]

- Go, and sin no more. The words Jesus spoke to the adulterer still hold power for us today. The benefits are beyond measure.[11]

- If you find yourself in an addiction, pattern of life, or behavior you can't seem to find release from, seek help immediately. There are many wonderful Christian counselors, medical doctors, pastors, and freedom ministry organizations that can help you with these life issues. Ask the Lord to lead you to the best one for you.[12]

Spiritual Warfare...

Most Bible Scholars agree that approximately one-third of Jesus' earthly ministry dealt with freeing people from demonic tyranny in their lives. This included demonic spirits of infirmity.[13]

To some degree, a good portion of illness is a direct fallout from our broken world and our enemy, the devil. We must consider this as we seek our own healing or healing for others. As we have been learning, walking with Jesus is just that—a walk. Just like a toddler and their first steps, we may stumble and fall a bit, but that shouldn't keep us from getting back on our feet and pressing forward and contending for the authentic in every area of our lives. In spiritual warfare, we will grow and gain experience with each step we take as the Holy Spirit leads us.

The devil is nothing like the Lord Almighty and can only be in one place at a time. He works through fallen spirits that do his bidding, but they are extremely limited beings except for what we allow them to do. When the Lord Jesus was on the cross, He destroyed all the weapons of the devil and his demonic spirits.[14] In turn, the Lord gave us His authority over these principalities and powers in His Name.[15]

> *Behold, I give you the authority to trample on serpents*
> *and scorpions, and over all the power of the enemy, and*
> *nothing shall by any means hurt you.*

> Luke 10:19

If you are uncertain to what degree the enemy is playing a part in a physical issue you are dealing with, ask the Lord Himself. Again, we are learning to hear His voice in our hearts and through His Word. What are you sensing? What is He saying?

However God is leading you to pursue His healing–through medicine, a natural or osteopathic route, no medical treatment, or a combination of any of these–don't discount the fact that you may be afflicted by the enemy to some degree.

The Bible tells us that we do not war against flesh and blood, but against the enemy. We battle these entities from our position in Christ in heavenly places in the spiritual realm.[16] How do we battle them? Dick Eastman, president of *Every Home for Christ*, writes about spiritual warfare in this manner:

> *Thus, prayer is not so much a weapon, or even a part of the armor, as it is the means by which we engage in the battle itself and purpose for which we are armed. To put on the armor of God is to prepare for battle. Prayer is the battle itself, with God's Word being our chief weapon employed against Satan during our struggle.*

We take our lead from the Lord Jesus Himself who rebuked or cancelled the enemy's work in people's lives. Employing the authority of the Name above all names, we speak Jesus' name directly to the spirit that is afflicting us or is afflicting the person we are praying for. In the authority of Jesus' name, we command that spirit to leave and never come back. It is helpful to back up our words with Scripture. In my situation, I spoke to the spirit of cancer out of Isaiah 41 that he was a non-existent thing in my life, in the name of Jesus!

If spiritual warfare is new to you, it is recommended that you don't attempt this on your own at first. Ask the help of spiritual leaders in your life and church to pray with you and for you.

Is anyone among you sick? Let him call for the elders of the church, and let them pray over him, anointing him with oil in the name of the Lord.

And the prayer of faith will save the sick, and the Lord will raise him up. And if he has committed sins, he will be forgiven.

James 5:14-15

The crux of spiritual warfare is found in the Lord's prayer:

Your kingdom come.
Your will be done
On earth as it is in heaven.

Matthew 6:10

We are inviting the rule of heaven to take place on earth in our situation. This applies to every area of our lives that needs God's healing touch. The Lord is always available to us and He has given us many tools through His Word and the Holy Spirit to see our victories secured in His glorious name.

9

God Alone

I have heard of You by the hearing of the ear,
But now my eye sees You.

Job 42:5

When we have genuinely sought the Lord for His healing touch, we have asked Him to search our hearts for any hidden hindrances, and we have come against sickness in Jesus' name, but healing still seems delayed, we then both stand firm in our faith and rest in Him.[1] We can wait upon Him for what He is going to do.

These are times when knowing God intimately is all that matters, and it is more than enough. We can rest in what we believe He has spoken to us and wait for His timing. And yes, Jesus truly does have timing that we may not understand, but He knows exactly what He is doing.[2]

The apostle Paul, who had prayed for and saw countless people healed physically, knew Jesus in the secret place. At one point in his life, Paul needed physical healing, too. He prayed to Jesus three times. Let's hear the Lord's reply to Paul…

> *And He said to me, "My grace is sufficient for you, for*
> *My strength is made perfect in weakness."*

Paul's response to what Jesus said…

> *Therefore most gladly I will rather boast in my*
> *infirmities, that the power of Christ may rest upon me.*
> *Therefore I take pleasure in infirmities, in reproaches, in*

needs, in persecution, in distresses, for Christ's sake.
For when I am weak, then I am strong"

2 Corinthians 12:9-10

We never learn if Paul received his physical healing or not. However, experiencing the all-sufficiency of God's grace was, to Paul, overwhelmingly more than enough.

As we wait on God's timing for our healing, we discover that the Old Testament also speaks often of *waiting* on the Lord, too. Waiting is usually the last thing we want to do, yet the Bible's word for waiting entails so much more than tapping our fingers on our watch and counting the minutes.

Wait on the LORD;
Be of good courage,
And He shall strengthen your heart;
Wait, I say, on the LORD!

Psalm 27:14

But those who wait on the LORD
Shall renew their strength;
They shall mount up with wings like eagles,
They shall run and not be weary,
They shall walk and not faint.

Isaiah 40:31

The Hebrew word *qavah* translated *wait* in these verses means *to wait for, look for, expect, and hope.*

Qavah is an active word, not a passive one. It is much like a waitperson serving you. As they wait on you, they are listening for what you desire or how you want something done, and we are doing the same with the Lord. We are waiting expectantly upon His desire or direction.[3] It also means *to gather together, to bind up, and to adhere to.*

To expectantly wait on God means *to lose yourself in Him*; to be so bound up with Jesus that you cannot be separated from Him. This changes the whole dynamic of our season of waiting in *any* area of our lives. Waiting on God changes what may seem negative at first to something that is oh so positive and we find ourselves hidden in Christ.[4]

We cannot earn, strive for, or try to coerce, or manipulate the Lord to move on our behalf.

I was once asked if we should demand God to heal us based upon Jesus' atoning work on the cross. Do you demand something from Someone you love, and Who loves You unconditionally? I think not. That seems more like testing God that Jesus advised the devil and us *not* to do.[5] Instead, let's directly command and demand our sickness to leave us in the authority of Jesus' name, including the influence of the devil, the author of almost all illness.[6]

It is probably not wise to insist on how healing should look. Again, we search God's Word to see the variety of ways the Lord ministered wholeness or what He required from people to take a step of faith or obedience to initiate recovery. Naaman's story from 2 Kings 5:1-15 is a perfect example of a person attempting to dictate to God how his healing should come and what limitations he would place upon God to procure his healing. Jesus invites us to come boldly to His throne of grace. Nevertheless, we come humbly knowing that He alone is our loving, omnipotent King, but we are mere dust before Him. In other words – what He says, goes!

We must be careful to discern when we might be placing *faith in our faith*, instead of trusting solely in Lord Jesus for healing. I have encountered this in many instances where people emphasized their healing instead of their relationship to Jesus by trying to say the right words, not acknowledging symptoms, or not accepting sound advice. If they slipped up and spoke anything contrary to a hard line of healing, they feared they were nullifying God's work. We can take a cue from the Apostle Paul that he was not afraid to name the reality of sickness.[7] We veer off course when we think our healing is predicated on saying the correct combination of words, like trying to get the tumblers in the right place to unlock something. This sounds a little more like witchcraft or manipulation than a real relationship and faith with our Father.

Yes, there *is* power in our words. Sometimes, these measures of what we say or do *are* very important as steps of obedience, but *as the Holy Spirit leads*. I often proclaimed the Bible verses the Lord gave me out loud over my body. I felt led by the Holy Spirit to directly speak to the cancer and the spirit of infirmity behind it, telling it to leave me in Jesus' All-Powerful Name. I kept sticky-notes near my work computer with scriptures that people gave me to remind myself of all Jesus was saying to me. I filled my mind with these words from His Word. However, I still held my life lightly in my hands, knowing He had the *final word* over everything about me.

Yet, no matter how long we have been a Christian, encountering Jesus by His all-sufficient grace keeps our eyes lifted toward Him. We will hear what He is doing and saying that will help us not to become fixated exclusively on being healed. Tremendous peace comes from this and our efforts cease. We will enter the place of rest He invites us into.[8]

Consider Shadrach, Meshach, and Abed-Nego from the Book of Daniel. Because these three faith heroes would not bow to the idol image of King Nebuchadnezzar, they faced imminent, fiery death. Their reply?

> *Shadrach, Meshach, and Abed-Nego answered and said to the king, "O Nebuchadnezzar, we have no need to answer you in this matter.*
>
> *If that is the case, our God whom we serve is able to deliver us from the burning fiery furnace, and He will deliver us from your hand, O king.*
>
> ***But if not**, let it be known to you, O king, that we do not serve your gods, nor will we worship the gold image which you have set up."*
>
> Daniel 3:16-18 (emphasis mine)

These three men placed their lives entirely upon God Almighty, no matter what happened to them. They were thrown into the fiery furnace and *delivered* without even a trace of smoke upon their clothing! Nevertheless, they sought to worship God Almighty more than they sought their physical wellbeing.

God Alone…

This is what the whole book of Job is about.

Honestly, before I experienced cancer, Job was my least favorite book in God's Word. I just didn't get it. I didn't like the narration of all the untold tragedy, and sickness that Job went through. I didn't understand all the anger, frustration, pleading, discussions, and praying to no avail. But then, God shows up. He was there all along, but Job and his friends missed Him entirely, and initially, I did too. Like them, I discussed and studied Him, but along with them, I *did not see Him.*

The miracle of Job's story is not his healing and restoration, but that He *intimately encountered the God of the universe.*

Just like Job, when we encounter the Lord, physical healing seems paltry at best. Healing pales in comparison to being in the Almighty's presence on a daily basis, even though that is often where physical wholeness is experienced. In fact, Job's physical healing isn't even mentioned in the story; it seems to become an irrelevant point. Nevertheless, it is implied later in the chapter when Job's losses are doubly restored, and we learn that Job died at an old age and full of days.[9]

I am not diminishing our desire to be completely healed. Nevertheless, our experiencing the Almighty is ever so much more glorious because it transforms *everything about everything* in our lives.

> *Then Job answered the LORD and said:*
>
> *"I know that You can do everything,*
> *And that no purpose of Yours can be withheld from You.*

You asked, 'Who is this who hides counsel without knowledge?'
Therefore I have uttered what I did not understand,
Things too wonderful for me, which I did not know

I have heard of You by the hearing of the ear,
But now my eye sees You.

Job 42:1-3, 5

When Heaven Calls...

When we draw close to Jesus in the joy of His presence, the lines between earth and heaven are blurred and fear ceases to have a grip upon us. Jesus came to destroy the power of death and destroy the fear of death itself.[10] Remember, we don't come to these times of just being with Him because we have all our ducks in a row or haven't sinned too badly in the recent past. We come into His presence because we are so needy and desperate, and we can't live apart from His touch.

He wants us to come and encounter Him as Job did, and He has extended the invitation to anyone who will accept.[11] There, with Him, a taste of heaven is made real for us and no longer becomes just a hope. The Holy Spirit does this because He is the guarantee of our inheritance in Christ both now and later,[12] and we can wait expectantly for what miracle He will do in our lives.

And sometimes, the miracle may be that Jesus is calling us home to be with Him.

Yesterday, a friend reminded me that all the promises of God are *yes*.

> *But God is faithful...For all the promises of God in Him are Yes, and in Him Amen, to the glory of God through us.*

2 Corinthians 1:18-20

Our Father will always fulfill His promises this side of heaven or in heaven itself.

When we have confidence that He has spoken to our hearts that we will be taking our leave of earth and heading Home, we can have His peace and joy, without fear, just like Connie and countless others have experienced. Paul further expresses this wondrous encounter of recognizing eternity in 2 Corinthians 4:16-5:8. Please take the time to read the entire text as I am only sharing a portion of it…

> *Therefore we do not lose heart. Even though our outward man is perishing, yet the inward man is being renewed day by day.*
>
> *For our light affliction, which is but for a moment, is working for us a far more exceeding and eternal weight of glory,*
>
> *while we do not look at the things which are seen, but at the things which are not seen. For the things which are seen are temporary, but the things which are not seen are eternal.*
>
> 2 Corinthians 4:16-18

Randy and I have a close friend who, at this moment, is in the care of hospice. His stage 4 pancreatic cancer has spread through his body. He initially sought the Lord for healing, and it still may take place. Yet, he recently felt tremendous peace that it *really is* his time to go home and be with King Jesus. His comfort and faith are as strong as ever, and he is enjoying the time he has with his family. His peace and joy are contagious, and this man has no fear. He is ready.

Some may say that is defeat. To my way of thinking, this is pure victory and glory. Jesus wins. Our friend wins. He has encountered the Lord GOD, and that is all that matters. He will be healed and made whole in Jesus' presence.

In Closing...

The Lord Jesus has so much for you to experience today, wherever this day finds you.

- There *is* healing in Him.

- Jesus has not changed.

- God's miracles are all around, and they still happen.

But there is so much more to discover in Him, the power of the Holy Spirit, and His Word. Be encouraged to seek the Lord. He will not disappoint.

Let the healing journey begin...

> *Now hope does not disappoint, because the love of God has been poured out in our hearts by the Holy Spirit who was given to us.*
>
> Romans 5:5

10

His Words

So then faith comes by hearing,
and hearing by the word of God.

Romans 10:17

God's Word, the Bible, is His guidebook, treasure map, oxygen tank, feast basket, weapon of war, instrument of healing, counselor, medicine bag, flashlight, and ultimately, His love letter to humanity.

As the verse above states, our faith is strengthened when we hear or read God's Word. The following Scriptures are only a *tiny portion* of what the Bible has to offer to position our hearts to receive His peace, joy, wisdom, love, power, and yes, healing.

I encourage you to look up the following passages in your own Bible, especially those verses where I only provide a shortened rendering. It will be helpful for you to read the entire passage for context and greater blessing.

Underline, meditate upon, and let the Holy Spirit speak from His Living Word to you and your situation.

My son, give attention to my words;
Incline your ear to my sayings.
Do not let them depart from your eyes;
Keep them in the midst of your heart;
For they are life to those who find them,
And health to all their flesh.

Proverbs 4:20-22

For Healing...

Held in His Hand – Isaiah 41:10-13 *(read through verse 19)*

> *Fear not, for I am with you; Be not dismayed, for I am your God. I will strengthen you, Yes, I will help you, I will uphold you with My righteous right hand.*

> *Behold, all those who were incensed against you Shall be ashamed and disgraced; They shall be as nothing,*

> *And those who strive with you shall perish.*

> *You shall seek them and not find them--Those who contended with you. Those who war against you Shall be as nothing, As a nonexistent thing.*

> *For I, the LORD your God, will hold your right hand, Saying to you, "Fear not, I will help you."*

Everlasting Arms – Deuteronomy 33:27 *(read verses 26-29)*

> *The eternal God is your refuge,*
> *And underneath are the everlasting arms;*
> *He will thrust out the enemy from before you,*
> *And will say, 'Destroy!'*

Health and Healing – Jeremiah 33:6 *(read verses 1-22)*

> *Behold, I will bring it health and healing; I will heal them and reveal to them the abundance of peace and truth.*

Give Life – Romans 8:11 *(read all of Romans 8)*

> *But if the Spirit of Him who raised Jesus from the dead dwells in you, He who raised Christ from the dead will also give life to your mortal bodies through His Spirit who dwells in you.*

Life – Psalm 118:17 *(read all of Psalm 118)*

> *I shall not die, but live,*
> *And declare the works of the LORD.*

By His Stripes We are Healed – Isaiah 53:5 *(read all of Isaiah 53)* Cross references: Matthew 8:17, 1 Peter 2:24

> *But He was wounded for our transgressions,*
> *He was bruised for our iniquities;*
> *The chastisement for our peace was upon Him,*
> *And by His stripes we are healed.*

Healing for Everyone – Matthew 8:16 *(read all of Matthew 8)*

> *When evening had come, they brought to Him many who were demon-possessed. And He cast out the spirits with a word, and healed all who were sick.*

Healing and Deliverance – Luke 6:17-19

> *And He came down with them and stood on a level place with a crowd of His disciples and a great multitude of people from all Judea and Jerusalem, and from the seacoast of Tyre and Sidon, who came to hear Him and be healed of their diseases,*
>
> *as well as those who were tormented with unclean spirits. And they were healed.*
>
> *And the whole multitude sought to touch Him, for power went out from Him and healed them all.*

Pursuing Jesus – Luke 8:48 *(read verses 40-48)*

> *And He said to her, "Daughter, be of good cheer; your faith has made you well. Go in peace."*

He is Willing – Luke 5:12-13 *(read verse 14)*

And it happened when He was in a certain city, that behold, a man who was full of leprosy saw Jesus; and he fell on his face and implored Him, saying, "Lord, if You are willing, You can make me clean."

Then He put out His hand and touched him, saying, "I am willing; be cleansed." Immediately the leprosy left him.

Ministry of Believers – Luke 9:1-2 *(read verses 1-6 and Luke 10:1-20)*

Then He called His twelve disciples together and gave them power and authority over all demons, and to cure diseases.

He sent them to preach the kingdom of God and to heal the sick.

Deliverance – 2 Corinthians 1:9-10 *(read verses 8-11)*

Yes, we had the sentence of death in ourselves, that we should not trust in ourselves but in God who raises the dead,

who delivered us from so great a death, and does deliver us; in whom we trust that He will still deliver us.

Recovery – Mark 16:18 *(read verses 14-20)*

They will take up serpents; and if they drink anything deadly, it will by no means hurt them; they will lay hands on the sick, and they will recover.

The Power of the Gospel – Acts 10:38 *(read verses 34-48)*

God anointed Jesus of Nazareth with the Holy Spirit and with power, who went about doing good and healing all who were oppressed by the devil, for God was with Him.

A Promise – Exodus 15:26

If you diligently heed the voice of the LORD your God and do what is right in His sight, give ear to His commandments and keep all His statutes, I will put none of the diseases on you which I have brought on the Egyptians. For I am the LORD who heals you.

The Lord, Our Defense – Psalm 91:9-10 *(read all of Psalm 91)*

Because you have made the LORD, who is my refuge,
Even the Most High, your dwelling place,

No evil shall befall you,
Nor shall any plague come near your dwelling;

Healing in His Wings – Malachi 4:2-3 *(read verse 1)*

"But to you who fear My name
The Sun of Righteousness shall arise
With healing in His wings;
And you shall go out
And grow fat like stall-fed calves.

You shall trample the wicked,
For they shall be ashes under the soles of your feet
On the day that I do this,"
Says the LORD of hosts.

Psalm 103:2-4 *(read all of Psalm 103)*

Bless the LORD, O my soul,
And forget not all His benefits:

Who forgives all your iniquities,
Who heals all your diseases,

Who redeems your life from destruction,
Who crowns you with lovingkindness and tender mercies

Healing for the Whole Person – 1 Thessalonians 5:23-24 *(read verses 15-24)*

> *Now may the God of peace Himself sanctify you completely; and may your whole spirit, soul, and body be preserved blameless at the coming of our Lord Jesus Christ.*

> *He who calls you is faithful, who also will do it.*

Have Spiritual Leaders Pray for You – James 14-15 *(read verses 15-24)*

> *Is anyone among you sick? Let him call for the elders of the church, and let them pray over him, anointing him with oil in the name of the Lord.*

> *And the prayer of faith will save the sick, and the Lord will raise him up. And if he has committed sins, he will be forgiven.*

Presenting Our Bodies to the Lord – Romans 12:1-2

> *I beseech you therefore, brethren, by the mercies of God, that you present your bodies a living sacrifice, holy, acceptable to God, which is your reasonable service.*

> *And do not be conformed to this world, but be transformed by the renewing of your mind, that you may prove what is that good and acceptable and perfect will of God.*

For Spiritual Warfare...

His Authority for You – Luke 10:18-19 *(read verses 1-20)*

> *And He said to them, "I saw Satan fall like lightning from heaven.*

Behold, I give you the authority to trample on serpents and scorpions, and over all the power of the enemy, and nothing shall by any means hurt you."

Strong in the Lord, His Armor – Ephesians 6:10-12 *(read verses10-20)*

Finally, my brethren, be strong in the Lord and in the power of His might.

Put on the whole armor of God, that you may be able to stand against the wiles of the devil.

For we do not wrestle against flesh and blood, but against principalities, against powers, against the rulers of the darkness of this age, against spiritual hosts of wickedness in the heavenly places.

Demonic Entities Defeated - Colossians 2:14-15 *(read verses 1-15)*

Having wiped out the handwriting of requirements that was against us, which was contrary to us. And He has taken it out of the way, having nailed it to the cross.

Having disarmed principalities and powers, He made a public spectacle of them, triumphing over them in it.

For This Purpose – 1 John 3:8b *(read verses 4-9)*

For this purpose the Son of God was manifested, that He might destroy the works of the devil.

Our Battle is in the Spirit – 2 Corinthians 10:3-5 *(read verses 1-6)*

For though we walk in the flesh, we do not war according to the flesh.

For the weapons of our warfare are not carnal but mighty in God for pulling down strongholds, casting down arguments and every high thing that exalts itself against the knowledge of God, bringing every thought into captivity to the obedience of Christ,

The Name Above Every Sickness – Philippians 2:9-11 *(read verses 5-11)*

Therefore God also has highly exalted Him and given Him the name which is above every name,

that at the name of Jesus every knee should bow, of those in heaven, and of those on earth, and of those under the earth,

and that every tongue should confess that Jesus Christ is Lord, to the glory of God the Father.

An Example – Acts 3:6 *(read verses 1-10)*

Then Peter said, "Silver and gold I do not have, but what I do have I give you: In the name of Jesus Christ of Nazareth, rise up and walk."

His Power Through Us – Ephesians 1:19-21 *(real all of Ephesians 1)*

And what is the exceeding greatness of His power toward us who believe, according to the working of His mighty power

which He worked in Christ when He raised Him from the dead and seated Him at His right hand in the heavenly places,

far above all principality and power and might and dominion, and every name that is named, not only in this age but also in that which is to come.

Speak to the Mountain – Matthew 21:21-22

So Jesus answered and said to them, "Assuredly, I say to you, if you have faith and do not doubt, you will not only do what was done to the fig tree, but also if you say to this mountain, 'Be removed and be cast into the sea,' it will be done.

And whatever things you ask in prayer, believing, you will receive.'

The Spirit of the Lord – Isaiah 59:19 *(read verses 16-21)*

So shall they fear
The name of the LORD from the west,
And His glory from the rising of the sun;
When the enemy comes in like a flood,
The Spirit of the LORD will lift up a standard against
him.

The Lord is With You - 2 Chronicles 20:17 *(read verses 1-30*

You will not need to fight in this battle. Position yourselves, stand still and see the salvation of the LORD, who is with you, O Judah and Jerusalem! Do not fear or be dismayed; tomorrow go out against them, for the LORD is with you.

Worship is Warfare – Psalm 149:6 *(read all of Psalm 149)*

Let the high praises of God be in their mouth,
And a two-edged sword in their hand,

Jesus' Abundant Life for You – John 10:10 *(read verses 1-18)*

The thief does not come except to steal, and to kill, and to destroy. I have come that they may have life, and that they may have it more abundantly.

Surrender to Jesus, then Resist – James 4:7 *(read through verse 10)*

Therefore submit to God. Resist the devil and he will flee from you.

We Have All We Need – Ephesians 1:3 *(read all of Ephesians 1)*

> *Blessed be the God and Father of our Lord Jesus Christ, who has blessed us with every spiritual blessing in the heavenly places in Christ*

Your Position in Christ – Ephesians 2:4-6 *(read all of Ephesians 2)*

> *But God, who is rich in mercy, because of His great love with which He loved us,*
>
> *even when we were dead in trespasses, made us alive together with Christ (by grace you have been saved),*
>
> *and raised us up together, and made us sit together in the heavenly places in Christ Jesus.*

What He Has Given Us – 2 Timothy 1:7

> *For God has not given us a spirit of fear, but of power and of love and of a sound mind.*

For His Presence...

Jesus, Our Example – Luke 6:12

> *Now it came to pass in those days that He went out to the mountain to pray. and continued all night in prayer to God.*

The Secret Place – Matthew 6:6 *(read all of Matthew 6)*

> *But you, when you pray, go into your room, and when you have shut your door, pray to your Father who is in the secret place; and your Father who sees in secret will reward you openly.*

The One Thing – Luke 10:39, 41-42 *(read verses 38-42)*

> *And she had a sister called Mary, who also sat at Jesus'
> feet and heard His word.*
>
> *And Jesus answered and said to her, "Martha, Martha,
> you are worried and troubled about many things.*
>
> *But one thing is needed, and Mary has chosen that good
> part, which will not be taken away from her."*

In His Presence – Psalm 16:11 *(read all of Psalm 16)*

> *You will show me the path of life;*
> *In Your presence is fullness of joy;*
> *At Your right hand are pleasures forevermore.*

The Beauty of the Lord – Psalm 27:4 *(read all of Psalm 27)*

> *One thing I have desired of the LORD,*
> *That will I seek:*
> *That I may dwell in the house of the LORD*
> *All the days of my life,*
> *To behold the beauty of the LORD,*
> *And to inquire in His temple.*

Thirsting for God - Psalm 63:1 *(read all of Psalm 63)*

> *O God, You are my God;*
> *Early will I seek You;*
> *My soul thirsts for You;*
> *My flesh longs for You In a dry and thirsty land*
> *Where there is no water.*

Secret Place of Shelter – Psalm 91:1-2 *(read all of Psalm 91)*

> *He who dwells in the secret place of the Most High*
> *Shall abide under the shadow of the Almighty."*
>
> *I will say of the LORD,*

"He is my refuge and my fortress;
My God, in Him I will trust."

Waiting (Qavah) on Him – Isaiah 40:31 *(read all of Isaiah 40)*

But those who wait on the LORD
Shall renew their strength;
They shall mount up with wings like eagles,
They shall run and not be weary,
They shall walk and not faint.

Pressing into Him – Philippians 3:12 *(read verses 12-14)*

Not that I have already attained, or am already
perfected; but I press on, that I may lay hold of that for
which Christ Jesus has also laid hold of me.

Abide in Jesus – John 15:7, 9, 11 *(read John 15:1-17)*

If you abide in Me, and My words abide in you, you will
ask what you desire, and it shall be done for you.

As the Father loved Me, I also have loved you; abide in
My love.

These things I have spoken to you, that My joy may
remain in you, and that your joy may be full.

The Holy Spirit...

The Promise of the Father – Luke 24:49 *(read next all of Acts 2)*

Behold, I send the Promise of My Father upon you;
but tarry in the city of Jerusalem until you are endued
with power from on high.

Pentecost – Acts 2:1, 4 *(read all of Acts 2)*

When the Day of Pentecost had fully come, they were all with one accord in one place.

And they were all filled with the Holy Spirit and began to speak with other tongues, as the Spirit gave them utterance.

Just Ask – Luke 11:11-13 *(read verses 9-13)*

If a son asks for bread from any father among you, will he give him a stone? Or if he asks for a fish, will he give him a serpent instead of a fish?

Or if he asks for an egg, will he offer him a scorpion?

If you then, being evil, know how to give good gifts to your children, how much more will your heavenly Father give the Holy Spirit to those who ask Him!

His Continuing Work – Acts 10:44-47 *(read all of Acts 10)*

While Peter was still speaking these words, the Holy Spirit fell upon all those who heard the word.

And those of the circumcision who believed were astonished, as many as came with Peter, because the gift of the Holy Spirit had been poured out on the Gentiles also.

For they heard them speak with tongues and magnify God. Then Peter answered,

"Can anyone forbid water, that these should not be baptized who have received the Holy Spirit just as we have?"

His Work in Us – Romans 8:15-17 *(read all of Romans 8)*

> *For you did not receive the spirit of bondage again to fear, but you received the Spirit of adoption by whom we cry out, "Abba, Father."*

> *The Spirit Himself bears witness with our spirit that we are children of God,*

> *and if children, then heirs – heirs of God and joint heirs with Christ, if indeed we suffer with Him, that we may also be glorified together.*

The Holy Spirit Within the Believer – John 7:37-39

> *On the last day, that great day of the feast, Jesus stood and cried out, saying, "If anyone thirsts, let him come to Me and drink.*

> *He who believes in Me, as the Scripture has said, out of his heart will flow rivers of living water."*

> *But this He spoke concerning the Spirit, whom those believing in Him would receive; for the Holy Spirit was not yet given, because Jesus was not yet glorified.*

The Power of the Resurrection Toward Us – Ephesians 1:18-20 *(read all of Ephesians 1)*

> *The eyes of your understanding being enlightened; that you may know what is the hope of His calling, what are the riches of the glory of His inheritance in the saints,*

> *and what is the exceeding greatness of His power toward us who believe, according to the working of His mighty power*

> *which He worked in Christ when He raised Him from the dead and seated Him at His right hand in the heavenly places,*

For Encouragement…

He Will See You Through - Isaiah 43:1-2 *(read all of Isaiah 43)*

> *But now, thus says the LORD, who created you, O Jacob,*
> *And He who formed you, O Israel:*
> *"Fear not, for I have redeemed you;*
> *I have called you by your name;*
> *You are Mine.*
>
> *When you pass through the waters, I will be with you;*
> *And through the rivers, they shall not overflow you.*
> *When you walk through the fire, you shall not be burned,*
> *Nor shall the flame scorch you.*

The Lord is My Shepherd – Psalm 23:1-2 *(read all of Psalm 23)*

> *The LORD is my shepherd;*
> *I shall not want.*
>
> *He makes me to lie down in green pastures;*
> *He leads me beside the still waters.*

Do Not Worry – Matthew 6:25-26 *(read all of Matthew 6)*

> *Therefore I say to you, do not worry about your life, what*
> *you will eat or what you will drink; nor about your body,*
> *what you will put on. Is not life more than food and the*
> *body more than clothing?*
>
> *Look at the birds of the air, for they neither sow nor reap*
> *nor gather into barns; yet your heavenly Father feeds*
> *them. Are you not of more value than they?*

More than Conquerors Because of His Love – Romans 8:37-39 *(read all of Romans 8)*

> *Yet in all these things we are more than conquerors*
> *through Him who loved us.*

For I am persuaded that neither death nor life, nor angels nor principalities nor powers, nor things present nor things to come,

nor height nor depth, nor any other created thing, shall be able to separate us from the love of God which is in Christ Jesus our Lord.

Cast All Your Cares Upon Him – 1 Peter 5:6-7 *(read through verse 11)*

Therefore humble yourselves under the mighty hand of God, that He may exalt you in due time,

casting all your care upon Him, for He cares for you.

He Hears Our Prayers – 1 John 5:14-15

Now this is the confidence that we have in Him, that if we ask anything according to His will, He hears us. And if we know that He hears us, whatever we ask, we know that we have the petitions that we have asked of Him.

He Will Answer Our Prayers Victoriously – John 16:24, 33 *(read all of John 16)*

Until now you have asked nothing in My name. Ask, and you will receive, that your joy may be full.

These things I have spoken to you, that in Me you may have peace. In the world you will have tribulation; but be of good cheer, I have overcome the world.

NOTE: Whenever you need encouragement, turn to any of the Psalms or the four Gospels detailing Jesus' life and ministry. You will always be encouraged.

Acknowledgements

Hey, this book couldn't have been written without a little help from my friends. These dear ones read and reread the manuscript and put in their two-cents and proofing finds. Thank you from the bottom of my heart:

Kareen Caragan, Janine Lucia, Janet Hayton, Linda Stanley, JoAnn Robbins, Raulna Yousling, Deb Brannan, and Jessica Villanueva.

All my love forever and thanks to Randy who formatted the text and to Alicen Curtis from i design for the most amazing and beautiful cover art.

Acknowledgements

Resources

Please note, that because books and ministries are mentioned here, I may not completely agree with all that they share. Nevertheless, the Lord has used each of these resources to speak into and encourage my life and faith.

Healing the Sick
T.L. Osborn

The Essential Guide to Healing:
Equipping All Christians to Pray for the Sick
Bill Johnson & Randy Clark

Why Am I Not Healed? (When God Promised)
Glen Berteau

New Spirit Filled Life Bible
Jack Hayford, Litt.D. Executive Editor

Foundations of Pentecostal Theology
Guy P. Duffield & Nathaniel M. Van Cleave

Your Battles Belong to the Lord:
Know Your Enemy and be More than a Conqueror
Joyce Meyer

The Spirit of the Lord is Upon Us
Leslie Keegel, D.D. DMin.

Penetrating the Darkness:
Discovering the Power of the Cross Against Unseen Evil
Jack Hayford, Litt.D.

The Bondage Breaker
Neil T. Anderson

They Shall Expel Demons:
What You Need to Know About Demons – Your Invisible Enemies
Derek Prince

The Beauty of Spiritual Language
Unveiling the Mystery of Speaking in Tongues
Jack Hayford, Litt.D.

The Holy Spirit in You
Derek Prince

Nine O'clock in the Morning
Dennis J. Bennett

Pneuma Life: Living in the Holy Spirit's Overflow
Sue Boldt

Intimate Friendship with God:
Through Understanding the Fear of the Lord
Joy Dawson

Sacred Rhythms:
Arranging Our Lives for Spiritual Transformation
Ruth Haley Barton

Refresh: Transformed Thoughts and Lives
Sue Boldt

Waking the Dead: The Secret to a Heart Fully Alive
John Eldredge

Living Hope Cancer Foundation
www.livinghopecancerfoundation.com

Healed of Cancer
Dodie Osteen

Notes

Chapter 1 – Cabin Retreat

[1] A computed tomography (CT or CAT) scan allows doctors to see inside your body. It uses a combination of X-rays and a computer to create pictures of your organs, bones, and other tissues. It shows more detail than a regular X-ray. www.webmd.com/cancer/what-is-a-ct-scan#1

[2] Acts 2:4, 1 Corinthians 14:4, This supernatural gift of the Holy Spirit is given to believers to encourage their faith and enhance their prayer and worship. A portion of Section II in this book is devoted to a short teaching on the power of the Holy Spirit in a Christian's life and steps to receiving this spiritual gift. For a more in-depth Bible study on the Holy Spirit and His gifts, see *Pneuma Life*, by Sue Boldt, available on Amazon.

[3] Philippians 4:7

[4] www.kidzone.ws/animals/monarch_butterfly.htm

[5] Jack W. Hayford, Litt.D., executive editor, *New Spirit Filled Life Bible* (Nashville, TN: Thomas Nelson, Inc. 2002) note for Isaiah 41:14-16

[6] Mitotane article – www.nejm.org/doi/full/10.1056/NEJMoa063360

[7] 1 John 4:18

[8] Isaiah 41:12

Chapter 2 – Once Again

[1] Matthew 14:36, Mark 8:23, Luke 4:39, Luke 17:14, John 5:8-9

[2] 2 Chronicles 16:9-13

[3] Spiros Zodhiates, Th.D, *Keyword Study Bible*, AMG International Publishers, Chattanooga, TN 37422 page 1505, Old Testament Lexical Aids #776

Chapter 3 – Held in His Hand

[1] A PET scan (also known as positron emission tomography and PET/CT) is a type of imaging study that can show doctors what's happening in your body and how it's working. It's different from an X-ray, CT, or MRI, providing important clues about how a disease is unfolding. www.webmd.com/a-to-z-guides/pet-scan#1

[2] Isaiah 41:12

[3] 1 Corinthians 12:9

Chapter 4 – Inviting Him In

[1] Psalm 23:6, Matthew 18:12, Luke 19:10

[2] Ezekiel 28, Luke 10:17-20

[3] Genesis 1-3

[4] Genesis 3:14-16, Romans 6:17-21 Here, God cursed the devil, who deceived Adam and Eve. The couple's disobedience caused their lives and all who would follow, to come under that same curse.

[5] Ephesians 2:1-3, Colossians 1:21

[6] Romans 5:12

[7] John 12:21, 1 John 5:19

[8] Isaiah 59:2, Romans 6:23

[9] John 3:16, Philippians 2:5-11, Hebrews 1:1-4

[10] Matthew 1:21, Hebrews 10:10-14

[11] John 1:12, John 3:16-17, John 17:3, Hebrews 2:14-15, 1 John 5:11

[12] 2 Corinthians 5:17, Romans 6:4, Romans 12:2, Revelation 21:5

[13] Colossians 1:27, Romans 5:5, John 3:3-7

[14] John 14:15-18, Hebrews 13:5-6, Deuteronomy 31:6

[15] John 14:12-13, Romans 8:31-39

[16] Psalm 16:11, John 15:9, Ephesians 3:16-20

[17] Luke 10:17-20, 1 John 3:8, Acts 3:6

[18] Hebrews 13:8

Chapter 5 – Power in His Word

[1] Deuteronomy 30:11-14

[2] Philippians 4:8, James 3:15-17

[3] 2 Timothy 3:16

[4] Luke 10:17-20, Ephesians 6:10-18

[5] John 12:31

[6] 1 John 5:2-3

[7] John 8:31-32

[8] John 1:14

[9] John 14:21

[10] Jack W. Hayford, Litt.D, Executive Editor, *New Spirit-Filled Life Bible*, *Third Edition* (Thomas Nelson, Nashville TN, 2018) Word Wealth at Matthew 4:4

[11] Hebrews 5:12-14

Chapter 6 – Holy Spirit Overflow

[1] Acts 2, 8:14-17, 9:17, 10:44-47, 19:1-7

[2] John 20:22, Luke 24:49, Acts 2:1-4

[3] Hebrews 13:8

[4] Acts 2:33

[5] There are many excellent Bible study books looking more in depth on Spirit baptism than I am giving here. For your own study, please look for books by Jack Hayford, Dennis Bennett. My own Bible study on the Holy Spirit, *Pneuma Life*, can be found on Amazon.

[6] 1 Corinthians 12:7-11

[7] 1 Corinthians 14:4,18, Ephesians 6:18, Jude 1:20

[8] John 1:12, Romans 8:9

[9] Matthew 14:22-31

[10] 1 Corinthians 14:13-15,18

[11] 1 Corinthians 14:14

Chapter 7 – Cultivating God's Presence

[12] Paul writes in Ephesians that we are to *be filled with the Spirit.* The Greek tense for *be filled* implies an ongoing manifestation of the Holy Spirit in a believer's life, not just a one-time event.

[1] Matthew 6:6, Luke 10:38-42, John 15:4-9, Psalm 23, Psalm 95:2

[2] Psalm 16:11, John 15:9, 1 Peter 1:8

[3] Psalm 46:10

[4] Luke 6:17-18, 13:11

[5] John 5:19

[6] Luke 4:1, John 5:19

[7] 2 Corinthians 5:21, Ephesians 1:7, Hebrews 10:19-22

[8] Romans 10:17, John 8:30-32

[9] Romans 12:1-2

[10] 2 Kings 5:10, Matthew 8:13, Mark 2:11, Luke 17:19

[11] Fasting food or something the Lord directs you to give up for a portion of time is a spiritual weapon in prayer. For a better understanding of the tool, please read Isaiah 58. *God's Chosen Fast,* by Arthur Wallis is a Christian classic on this subject.

[12] The work of the devil and his minions in this world is the subject of much of the Bible, however, that is not the focus of this short book. I do believe it is imperative that every believer know about our adversary and even more crucial, all that Jesus has given us to defeat him. There are several

great books to aid you in your Bible study about spiritual warfare. Please see the resource list of at the end of this book.

[13] James 4:8

[14] 1 Thessalonians 5:17, Ephesians 6:18, Jude 20

[15] Exodus 33:11, Psalms 27, 63, Luke 10:38-42

[16] Romans 8:15-17

[17] Wayne Cordeiro, The Divine Mentor (Grand Rapids, MI: Bethany House Publishers, 2007) page 109

[18] Jeremiah 30:2

[19] Psalm 22:3

[20] Randy Remington, President: International Church of the Foursquare Gospel, *Converge Event*, Santa Clarita, CA – September 23-24, 2019

[21] 1 Corinthians 14:26. This verse describes the many ways the Lord may speak to us.

[22] Romans 12:1-2

[23] Isaiah 26:3, John 16:22

Chapter 8 – When Healing is Delayed

[1] Luke 17:5 Mark 9:24

[2] Psalm 139:23-24

[3] Unbelief: Mark 6:5-6, Matthew 13:58, Unforgiveness: Matthew 6:14-15,

[4] Mayo Clinic, *Stress Symptoms: Effects on Your Body and Behavior,* www.mayoclinic.org/healthy-lifestyle/stress-management/in-depth/stress-symptoms/art-20050987. Johns Hopkins Medicine, *Forgiveness: Your Health Depends on It*, www.hopkinsmedicine.org/health/wellness-and-prevention/forgiveness-your-health-depends-on-it

[5] Isaiah 61:1-7, Luke 4:18-19

[6] Hebrews 4:14

[7] Deuteronomy 30:14-20, Psalm 27:11, Romans 5:17

[8] 1 John 1:9

[9] Ephesians 1:7, Colossians 1:14, Hebrews 10:10

[10] Romans 8:1, Ephesians 2:7-9

[11] John 8:11-12

[12] 1 Corinthians 10:13, Hebrews 2:17-18, Hebrews 4:14-16

[13] Matthew 17:15-18, Mark 9:17, Luke 13:11

[14] Colossians 2:14-15

[15] Acts 3:6

[16] Ephesians 2:6

Chapter 9 – God Alone

[1] Ephesians 6:13-18, Hebrews 4:9-10

[2] John 11

[3] Psalm 123:2

[4] Psalm 123:2

[5] Luke 4:9-12

[6] Acts 3:6, 16:18

[7] 2 Timothy 4:20

[8] Matthew 11:28-30, Hebrews 4:1-10

[9] Job 42:10,16,17

[10] Hebrews 2:14-15

[11] Revelation 3:20, John 3:16

[12] 2 Corinthians 1:22, 2 Corinthians 5:1-6 (These verses speak directly to the Holy Spirit as our guarantee for heaven), Ephesians 1:14

Made in the USA
Las Vegas, NV
21 December 2022

63759023R00066